"Steve's book, *Alongsider Coaching*, is exactly what it says it is. Jesus chose His twelve disciples to be with them. That is exactly what Steve has given us in this book... insight into how to be with people in a manner that reminds me of the way Jesus did it. The stories at the end of each chapter are worth the price of the book in helping the coachee to find themselves in a non-threatening way in the narrative. Thanks Steve for a job well done!"

**Richard E. Bush, DMin., Director of Coaching
for the Christian and Missionary Alliance**

"There is no greater combination than doing something that Jesus commanded us to do and doing it the way He modeled for us. By highlighting the act of making disciples through coaching, Steve Diehl has written a book with the potential to change the lives of people who may never even read it! That's amazing!"

**Tim Keller, Pastor and Regional
Coach, Carlisle Alliance Church**

"This book will inspire you to be a coach and to get a coach. Passing on to others the things that you have learned from the Lord is a great blessing. The Lord Jesus made disciples through personal relationships. That is still the pattern today."

**Keith Skelton, Retired Pastor and
Speaker, Edinburgh, Scotland**

Alongsider Coaching

The Art of Walking Alongside

Dr. Steven L. Diehl

LHP

Alongsider Coaching

Published by:
LifeHouse Publishing
P.O. Box 2825
Peoria, Arizona 85380
www.lifehousepub.com

ISBN 978-0-9839409-1-3

TABLE OF CONTENTS

INTRODUCTION

God said in Genesis 2:18, "It is not good for the man to be alone." Those words are often used in the context of marriage relationships, but the application is broader in scope. God cares about all relationships. People are not meant to be alone. You need other people, and other people need you. You were not created for isolation. Moses had Aaron. Paul had Barnabas. Timothy had Paul. Paul and Luke were traveling companions and fellow workers (Phil. 1:24; Col. 4:14; 2 Tim. 4:11). Ruth had Naomi, or Naomi had Ruth. It is reciprocal. Priscilla and Aquila. David and Jonathan. Jesus sent them out in pairs. Who is walking with you?

You were also created for a purpose. "And God blessed them, and God said to them, 'Be fruitful and multiply'" (Gen. 1:28a, Revised Standard Version). That early command of God is about more than simply having children. It is also about reproducing a spiritual family by investing in other people and making disciples. Who are you walking with?

When our two sons became teenagers, my wife and I knew we had to make some shifts in our parenting strategies. We knew that it would not fly to say, "No, because I said so and I'm bigger." If we were going to prepare our sons for life, there would need to be some adjustments in our approach to growing our beloved children. We knew intuitively that we had to do more listening and asking good questions than giving orders, directives, or uninvited advice. We recognized the need to give them freedom to learn from mistakes. We needed to help them mature rather than force them to grow up. We needed to help them figure out God's grain and texture in their lives. We needed to apply coaching skills in our parenting.

I cannot say that I was naturally gifted with the skills of a coaching parent, nor did I excel at it, but I became passionate about the idea of providing opportunities for them to try new things in order to discover what they were good at and who they were. Although "coaching" wasn't a term I would have used at the beginning, this was a season of life that sparked a journey toward what it means to help others grow up in Christ by walking alongside with relational encouragement.

When I type the word "alongsider," it doesn't pass the spell checker. My processer underlines it with an annoying squiggly red line. It does look a bit odd, but it is not at odds with the Bible and it is not a new concept. Walking alongside others is exemplified and underlined in the Scriptures. My hope is that this book will encourage you to be more intentional about coming alongside other people to encourage them as you model Christ-like characteristics.

Coaching is a common term these days. It is a word that describes how Jesus made disciples, walking with people along the journey of life. It is something He invites us to do with others.

Coaching is more of an art than a science. If my goal was to explain all the steps for doing it, alongsider coaching would be less artistic and creative. So, my hope is to create some sparks and offer some catalytic tools to get you going. My desire is to give you some paintbrushes, paint, and techniques that can thrust you into the joy of painting life into another person. That kind of painting puts you in the center of God's creative activity.

Coaching is a discipline that is challenging to articulate because, by its very nature, coaching is about relationships and walking in journey with others. Relational coaching techniques cannot be fully captured in writing, because life happens.

That being said, there are some insights and skills which can be cultivated so that when opportunity arises, a life to life alongsider coaching moment can be embraced.

Most of us have experienced the joy of a relationship where we grew because of someone's influence. Many of us can point to significant moments where someone we respected spoke into our lives or asked a powerful question to help us discover something which launched us into a life-changing decision. People who have been in our lives in that way are a gift and a blessing.

This book is meant to be an encouragement to those interested in coaching and to the many people who pray for and walk alongside others in quiet but meaningful relationships. Many are those who are serving God by walking intentionally alongside other people without a lot of public attention or recognition. That kind of walk honors God and needs to be multiplied. Some of you might be older. You have a story to tell. Tell it. Younger people need to hear it as you walk with them and take interest in them. If you are walking with Jesus you have things to tell the next generation (Ps. 48:13).

Seasons of significant growth for me have involved people who were willing to come alongside with truth, experience, and encouragement. I look back with gratitude for those who have taken the time to speak the truth in love, asking powerful questions to help me discover God's will, giving me the gift of a caring ear. This book is written with the hope of inspiring and mobilizing you to become an alongsider coach and walk with a coach, recognizing other people as God's gift for flexing your relational anti-isolation muscles.

I have a dream that every follower of Christ might experience the fulfillment, joy, and thrill of alongsider coaching. What if every church was filled with people willing to be alongsider coaches as a way to help others in the journey of following Jesus? What if every emerging leader had a coach walking alongside, helping in the preparation for future service? This book is an attempt to paint a picture of what alongsider coaching can look like.

Jesus invites us, "Come, follow me, and I will make you fishers of men" (Matt. 4:19). Jesus also said, "Don't be afraid; from now on you will catch men" (Luke 5:10). The response of those first disciples is inspiring. "So they pulled their boats up on shore, left everything and followed him" (Luke 5:11). May I encourage you to leave your nets and boats on the shore (and whatever else you naturally trust in to float through life) and follow Jesus as you consider His invitation to become a fisher of people. Alongsider coaching is about drawing people into a legacy and building a legacy that points to Jesus.

CHAPTER 1

ALONGSIDING

The presence of God is the central fact of Christianity.
At the heart of the Christian message is God Himself
waiting for His redeemed children to push in to conscious
awareness of His presence.
~A. W. Tozer~

Jesus showed up as two of His followers were walking along the road to a place called Emmaus. It was the same day as His resurrection. As they were walking and talking about everything that had happened, the Bible says that Jesus "drew near" (Luke 24:15b). He walked with them.

Jesus asked them, "What is this conversation that you are holding with each other as you walk?" (Luke 24:17). You might paraphrase that, "Hey guys, what are you talking about? What is the story?" His question stopped them in their tracks. They stood still, with their faces downcast in sadness. The events of that day had imprinted dark images in their minds, memories which threatened their hope. A man named Cleopas answered the question with a question. He inquired with wonder, "Are you only a visitor to Jerusalem and do not know the things that have happened there in these days?" They wondered how this man whom they didn't recognize as the risen Christ could possibly not know about the trials, beatings, and suffering of their leader.

Jesus followed up His powerful question, which the followers had answered with a question, with another question (that is a lot of questions), "What things?" (Luke 24:19).

Listening and asking good questions is what coaching looks like. I believe Jesus was intentionally modeling something powerful and profound. He gave us a picture of alongsider coaching.

At the end of the book of Matthew, with summarizing words before the ascension, Jesus invited His followers to go and make disciples of all nations (Matt. 28:18-20). The question that we often wrestle with is, "How do we do that?"

It would certainly make sense to do it like Jesus did it. He walked with twelve guys and stepped into teachable, coachable moments. His alongsider coaching example is inspiring, insightful, and encouraging, and serves as the inspiration and foundation of this book. Furthermore, when you embrace alongsider coaching relationships as a way to make disciples, you can be assured of God's empowering presence in the process. "And surely I am with you always, to the very end of the age" (Matt. 28:20b).

What is Coaching?

What comes to mind when you hear the word "coaching?" For most of us, "coaching" brings some sport to mind. You can never take an analogy, illustration, or word picture too far, but talking about coaching with sports in view is appropriate. For the sports coach, the players are the focus and the center of energy. The coach is on the sideline as the encourager. The coach observes, gives feedback, advocates, encourages, and gets excited about the players on the field. He or she celebrates successes and helps players to learn from mistakes.

For some of us, the term brings undesirable memories of people who did more yelling than anything else. I remember coaches who wouldn't let me off the bench. I've had coaches who put me in the wrong spot where I wasn't operating from my strengths. Some coaches in my life seemed more interested in their wins and personal success than team dynamics or growth and development of the players. Some coaches have not been good models of what effective coaching looks like.

The term "coaching" should elicit memories of special people who called out the best in you. The best coaches may be people who didn't know they were coaching you. They may have been encouraging you by relating in an advocate role, hearing your heart and helping you to be all that you can be. The kind of coaching we are talking about in this book involves coming alongside, in the power of the Holy Spirit, to help people discover and embrace God's will and calling. No athlete would expect to improve his game or participate in a sport without a coach. Nor can we become all that we can be in Christ without spiritual coaching. Alongsider coaching is really about discipleship as people follow Jesus with others.

> *Coming alongside, in the power of the Holy Spirit, to help people discover and embrace God's will and calling.*

When the topic of coaching comes up, my mind often defaults to football. I had some very good coaches during my football years. Growing up on the windy plains of Northern Illinois, my high school football team was the Freeport Pretzels. You read that right, the Pretzels. Opposing teams had fun with that, "Twist 'em, turn 'em, salt 'em, crumble them." We had to work hard at winning in order to keep our dignity. We needed good coaching to be winners. You are also positioned to see a need for prayer when curses are directed in your direction.

By the way, did you know that pretzels were invented by a European Monk who wanted to remind his students to pray? Consider the basic shape the next time you enjoy one of these salty treats, the image of cupped hands as a symbol of prayer. Prayer is a very important component of an alongsider coaching relationship. Staying in tune with God as the head coach is critical.

Whether it is football or another sport, the idea of coaching sparks athletic images. Maybe it's an individual sport like ice skating, or perhaps games like baseball or soccer where team play is more pronounced. Biblical coaching means people following Jesus are on the field, with coaches encouraging them to become all they can be.

The coach helps participants to see the bigger picture and warns of dangers on the fields of life. Knowing when to offer advice and counsel is crucial to effective alongsider coaching. Often the coach suggests strategies and plays to accomplish victories in the advance of the kingdom of light, defeating the kingdom of darkness with God-empowered conquests which spark celebration. Proper equipment is necessary (Eph. 6:10-18), and prayer is essential (Col. 4:2).

Coaching expresses itself in many different ways. Sometimes coaching is formalized, often it is spontaneous, but always it is rooted in relationship. There are also different categories of coaching. A defensive coach on a football team will apply different techniques than a baseball pitching coach. A hockey coach will need strengths that are different than a volleyball coach. A coach in a corporate supervisory role will approach coaching in a different way than a peer coach in a nonprofit organization. A relationship with a life coach will look different than a coach helping you with a particular skill. Sometimes coaching is directive, "do this," "try this," but it's also about drawing out the best from each player on the field.

So, what is alongsider coaching? It is, in essence, Christ-centered relational multiplication that happens as we walk alongside others. God uses people to reach people. God uses people to disciple people. In this book we are hoping to encourage coaching as the way to multiply life. To coach someone is

God uses people to disciple people.

to come alongside to encourage, pray for, assist, resource, direct, and equip another follower of Jesus to embrace God's purposes on purpose. It is life on life, it is partnering power, and it is full of opportunity to make a difference.

Alongsider Encouragement

People need encouragement. That is why the Bible says that we should encourage one another daily (Heb. 3:13). The world can be a very discouraging place, full of stuff that could bring fear, broken dreams, dashed hopes, and fractured relationships. People need to be filled with courage. Alongsider coaches can be God's provision to help people courageously embrace God's dream for them, with renewed hope to face life head on.

> *Alongsider coaches can be God's provision to help people courageously embrace God's dream for them.*

In Acts 4:36, Barnabas is introduced as the one whose name means "son of encouragement." When all others held a great distrust for Paul after his conversion on the Damascus Road (Acts 9), Barnabas the encourager presented him to the apostles. He told them how Saul (Paul's Jewish name), on his journey, had seen the Lord. He explained how God had spoken to Saul, and how in Damascus he had preached fearlessly in the name of Jesus (Acts 9:27). For Barnabas to position himself in that way must have been very encouraging to Paul.

Barnabas came alongside Paul and advocated for him. Barnabas not only made himself available to establish a coaching bond with Paul, he stuck with him. He encouraged Paul forward into doing what God was inviting him to do. Barnabas was willing, in humility, to thrust Paul beyond himself and into the spotlight of God's calling. He co-ministered with Paul for some time, but Paul's leadership potential then reached the point where it needed to be released.[1]

It is no accident that a shift is seen in the book of Acts, from "Barnabas and Saul" (Acts 11:26, 30; 12:25; 13:2) to "Paul and Barnabas" (Acts 13:42). This is a marked transfer of leadership from Barnabas in first seat to Paul in the lead. As we come to Acts 13:9, this is the first time that we see Paul clearly taking the lead ahead of Barnabas. By Acts 13:13, Paul is so much in the lead that Barnabas is not even mentioned, and from 14:42 on, when both are mentioned together, Paul is usually in the foremost position. Through Barnabas we discover some biblical foundations for alongsider coaching. It incorporates encouragement, advocates for people, builds trust, and calls out the best in the person to be coached. At some point this might mean positioning the other person ahead of oneself. That takes courage and it is encouraging.

> *It incorporates encouragement, advocates for people, builds trust, and calls out the best in the person to be coached.*

Jesus, in a sense, modeled this kind of encouragement on that road to Emmaus. As Luke recorded it, "And their eyes were opened, and they recognized Him. And He vanished from their sight" (Luke 24:31). He walked with them, asked some powerful questions, listened to them, explained the Scriptures to them, then disappeared so they could be empowered and encouraged to walk forward.

On that road to Emmaus (Luke 24:13ff), Jesus taught a powerful revelation of His person. He showed how everything in the Bible pointed to Him as Lord and Savior, but that was only after He asked several powerful questions and then listened to their hearts. As soon as they recognized Him, He disappeared. Leading up to the walking sermon and communion fellowship meal with them was a wonderful depiction of alongsiding. True alongsider coaching points beyond the coach to the person of Jesus. We decrease that He might increase. We disappear that He might more fully appear on the radar of those seeking to follow Him. When people see more of Jesus and less of us, that is the kind of alongsider coaching that fills people with courage.

Barnabas was a powerful role model of what it looks like to be available for alongsider coaching. He listened to the voice of the Holy Spirit, and he came alongside to advocate for the advance of a coaching relationship that made a kingdom impact. Barnabas was an alongsider coach who was one of God's provisions to move Paul onto a ministry field that changed the world.

Having had a coach in Barnabas, Paul multiplied himself as a coach for Timothy. In 2 Timothy 1:2, Paul calls Timothy "my dear son." Although there was probably a tone of coming into the kingdom as a spiritual son, it's not a stretch to say that Paul became a coach for Timothy. Paul's epistles are full of coaching words that were most likely written reminders of what he had encouraged and affirmed in person. He reminded Timothy of his love and concern for him (1 Tim. 1:2; 2 Tim. 1:2). Paul was thankful for their friendship and partnership (2 Tim. 1:3-5). He reminded Timothy to fan into flames his gift (2 Tim. 1:6), affirmed his knowledge of the Holy Scriptures (2 Tim. 3:15), urged him to pray (1 Tim. 2:1-7), charged him to fight the good fight of the faith (1 Tim. 6:11), and encouraged him not to let others look down on him because he was young (1 Tim. 4:12). Timothy, then, was encouraged to multiply himself by investing in others who would also be willing to invest in others (2 Tim. 2:1-3, 3:14-17; 1 Cor. 4:17). These are foundational biblical qualities of an alongsider coaching relationship that encourages.

What Alongsider Coaching is Not

Coaching is not the same as mentoring. A mentoring relationship is generally longer term and accomplished by various means which may not include a deliberate relational component. I have been mentored by people I didn't have a relationship with, including authors and preachers who wouldn't know my name.

In a coaching relationship, the person of focus is the coachee, not the coach. Coaching also has a different center of gravity. The coachee is the pilot in training, with the coach sitting in the co-pilot seat to encourage, train, and equip. In a mentoring relationship, by contrast, the center of gravity is normally in the mentor. Although a mentor may utilize coaching techniques, the mentor is normally the person in the pilot seat, with the mentoree in the co-pilot seat to observe and learn. This distinction is important to keep in view.

Coaching is also distinct from teaching, at least in the traditional sense. I was a classroom teacher for a number of years, and discovered that teaching in the classroom was mostly curriculum driven. There is certainly still a place for teacher led instruction, because certain kinds of information are best taught in groups with a leader dispensing needed training. But not everything can be learned in the classroom, and many things are better caught as life happens than taught in a formalized setting. Alongsider coaching compliments other forms of instruction and addresses life issues that can't be taught in a larger group situation.

Coaching is also not the same thing as counseling. The focus of a counselor is often to use the past to bring wellness and wholeness in the present. Coaching is about helping a person launch from the present into a brighter future. Effective counseling requires a particular skill set and specialized training. Not everyone can be a counselor. But most of us can develop coaching skills and be empowered by God to walk alongside others.

Coaching at its core is about relationship. There needs to be a significant relational component with coaching. Just for emphasis, let this be echoed and accented—COACHING IS ABOUT RELATIONSHIP. In the context of alongsider relationships, there is incredible potential for life transformation to happen. Coaching should focus on relationship, keeping in view the needs of the individual. There isn't a cookie-cutter approach to coaching relationships. Every person who is being coached is an individual, and a "one-size-fits-all" approach is neither wise nor productive. Coaching is relational and not institutional or curriculum driven. When you think, *coaching*, think *relationship*.

> When you think, coaching, think relationship.

When I was in high school, the varsity football coach lived right down the street from us. I knew him relationally, as a neighbor, before I knew him as a coach. I trusted him and respected him. I was receptive to his coaching and proactive about his input in my life because his coaching was rooted in relationship. He wasn't a mentor or teacher or counselor, he was a coach.

Helping People to Discover Their Grain

My father-in-law is gifted in working with wood. He has, for a number of years now, fashioned everything from oak toy boxes to cherry and maple coat trees and lecterns. The time, materials, and intense concentration required for his fine work of carpentry may not be fully grasped by those who have never endeavored to work with wood. The labors of a carpenter often go unappreciated by the inattentive eye. Much of the craftsman's character is hidden and sealed within the grain.

The transformation of raw materials into a unique, hand-crafted work of art is worthy of celebration and praise.

God shapes and fashions us as we submit to His hand. He has just the right tools to use on the raw material of His own creation. We are blocks of wood with fascinating potential as we intentionally place ourselves in His woodshop at the altar of His workbench. Can you look back on times of hammering and sanding, not understanding the pains at the time but thankful today for the results? He is still working on my rough edges, and I'm thankful that He knows His work. The final product will be according to His plans and for HIS pleasure and glory.

What a waste it would be if His masterful work in our lives went unappreciated. Alongsider coaching can help His fingerprints to be revealed within the grain. "The Lord God formed the man from the dust of the ground and breathed into his nostrils the breath of life." (Gen. 2:7) "For you make me glad by your deeds, oh Lord; I sing for joy at the works of your hands." (Ps. 92:4) Following Jesus means being fashioned by divine processes for His perfect purposes.

We get a good picture in the Bible of what God desires in Romans 8:28-29a, "And we know that in all things God works for the good of those who love him, who have been called according to his purpose. For those God foreknew he also predestined to be conformed to the likeness of his Son." To engage in alongside coaching is to help others discover God's grain in their lives and give Him the glory as He shapes them to become more and more like Jesus.

CHAPTER 2

WHAT DOES THE BIBLE SAY ABOUT IT?

As iron sharpens iron, so one man sharpens another.
~Proverbs 27:17~

"Coaching" is not a word that you will find in the Bible. However, there is a strong biblical basis for alongsider coaching. God's perspective on relational alongsider coaching can be found in the opening pages of Scripture. A wonderful relationship is described at the beginning of time for humankind, unfolding in the creation story. It was marked by an intimate, open, loving fellowship with the living God, with all that could be imagined as the ultimate friendship. God was the Creator, the Lord of the universe, all-powerful over everything He created. At the same time, He was a friend of the first human beings. He was above all, and yet He walked in fellowship with humans. As a friend and as the Lord, He embodied the character of the ultimate spiritual and relational coach. God walked with Adam and Eve in a loving relationship marked by closeness, trust, respect, and unhindered love.

How do we know these things? Jesus came to redeem and restore that which was lost (Luke 19:10). That includes the broken relationship with God. Through faith in Christ, a friendship is repaired. Fellowship with God becomes a restored reality. John fifteen puts color to the picture of a friendship with God, "Greater love has no one than this, that he lay down his life for his friends. You are my friends if you do what I command. I no longer call you servants, because a servant does not know his master's business. Instead, I have called you friends, for everything that I learned from my Father I have made known to you" (John 15:13-16). Jesus demonstrated true love in going to the cross in our place to restore us to a place of friendship with God, intimate fellowship with the Father.

Alongsider coaching helps people discover God's will as revealed in the Bible, enabling the embrace of His purpose on purpose. It is fascinating that the first words spoken to man invested purpose, encouragement, and challenge: "God blessed them and said to them, 'Be fruitful and increase in number; fill the earth and subdue it. Rule over the fish in the sea and the birds in the sky and over every living creature that moves on the ground'" (Gen. 1:28). In simple terms, God was commanding them to go and be what He had created them to be and do what He had created them to do. It is not a stretch to say that there are key coaching components in this first command.

Coaching also helps people experience God's provision. In Genesis one, God followed up His first command with a second one: "Then God said, 'I give you every seed-bearing plant on the face of the whole earth and every tree that has fruit with seed in it. They will be yours for food'" (Gen. 1:29). After inviting them to go forth and be fruitful and do what He created them to do, God was informing these first humans of His provision to accomplish His commands. This is another important element of alongsider coaching; helping those in a coaching relationship to discover God's provision for the journey of His calling. As these beginning pages of Scripture reveal, God has a purpose for each person, He provides everything necessary for accomplishing that purpose, and no one is alone on the journey. A coach can help a person hear God's voice, know His will,

> *Coaching also helps people experience God's provision.*

and engage His personal calling toward fruitful living for His eternal glory. God's will and calling come with His provision.

In Genesis chapter two, a warning from God was expressed: "And the Lord God commanded the man, 'You are free to eat from any tree in the garden; but you must not eat from the tree of the knowledge of good and evil, for when you eat of it you will certainly die'" (Gen. 2:16). This was a strong admonition. It was the raising of the red flag. It was a strict prohibition, the Father knowing what would happen with an act of disobedience.

Genesis chapter three happened. The first humans disobeyed. They made their own choice rather than God's choice. Relationships were severed and the destructive power of sin brought the great hurricane we know as the fall of man. A biblical foundation of the coaching model must include the component of knowing when to raise the red flag of warning. Alongsider coaching helps people become aware of dangers, weaknesses, and pitfalls in their own lives as they align themselves with biblical truth.

When the curse came with the fall of mankind, God provided what was necessary once again. He made the first sacrifice in providing garments of skin to clothe Adam and Eve (Gen. 3:21). To provide garments of skin, an animal had to die. Death was required to bring restored and renewed life. God provided a sacrifice then, and an even greater sacrifice at the cross.

Death was required to bring restored and renewed life.

Throughout the Old Testament God continued to provide for His people, even when they failed to listen and obey. Even when they ignored His warnings, God took care of His people. He rescued them, appointed leaders, and ultimately provided salvation and hope in the person of the Lord Jesus Christ.

The Example of Jesus

It is not a stretch to say that Jesus was (and is) the most profound spiritual coach that ever dwelt among us. He is the ultimate life coach. He coached twelve men, walking alongside them in abundant life. He taught the masses, but He trained the disciples as the coach of coaches. Relational ministry multiplication was how He mobilized and equipped the first disciples.

Jesus invited twelve guys to walk with Him through the classroom of life. He modeled the kind of relational investment that is crucial to building disciples who build disciples. In his book, *Christian Coaching*, Gary Collins explains, "He was a role model to them, showed them the way to go, observed their progress, corrected their misunderstandings, and gently encouraged them to go out on their own. Like any good coach, He gave them feedback and reevaluated their performances."[2]

Jesus carefully guided His discipleship team forward, drawing out their strengths and coaching them as they journeyed together. Their lives changed through the dynamics of relationship. Umidi summarizes Jesus' coaching role:

> It has become too easy to simply read what the gospels say but miss the point that what is said has an experiential, relational context—the essence of transformational coaching. Much of the key leadership and personal development for the disciples happened in coaching-type exchanges with Jesus after the sermons and teachings (Matt. 13:34-36).[3]

Jesus used questions, dialogue, stories, and healthy discussions as He walked alongside His followers. He also challenged, gave advice, and taught. However, even His teaching utilized coaching principles. Consider His "sermon" on

> *Jesus used questions, dialogue, stories, and healthy discussions as He walked alongside His followers.*

the mount (Matt. 5). You just can't look at that scene through a typical Sunday school classroom lens. They sat on a mountainside, breathing in fresh air, perhaps the sound of a gentle breeze blowing through the grass as Jesus taught. He used questions. "But if the salt loses its saltiness, how can it be made salty again?" (Matt. 5:13b). "If you love those who love you, what reward will you get? Are not even the tax collectors doing that? And if you greet only your own people, what are you doing more than others? Do not even pagans do that?" (Matt. 5:46-47). That sounds to me like teaching that utilized a conversational style with questions to draw out deeper lessons, setting the stage for alongsider coaching as they left that scene and journeyed forward.

Biblical Coaching Skills

When you see a picture of a man on his knees holding a ring and looking into the eyes of a woman, you know a question has been asked. He is waiting for a response, listening for an answer. Asking and listening is what coaching looks like.

When you see someone dribbling a basketball, you know what game is being played. Dribbling is a fundamental skill to the sport of basketball. Listening is to coaching what

> *Listening is to coaching what dribbling is to basketball.*

dribbling is to basketball and a marriage proposal is to a wedding. Effective listening is an important basic skill for alongsider coaching, and it is biblical.

Jesus modeled and taught effective listening. First and foremost, He listened to and heard from the Father (John 8:38-40). As He listened vertically, He was also listening horizontally to those around Him. When Jesus heard the message from the centurion asking Him to heal the servant, Jesus listened: "When Jesus heard this, he was amazed at him, and turning to the crowd following him, he said, 'I tell you, I have not found such great faith even in Israel'" (Luke 7:9-10).

Jesus coached His disciples in the importance and development of good listening skills. He encouraged them to be listeners (Matt. 13:18; 15:10; 21:33; Mark 4:3; 7:14). When He sent out the seventy-two, He instructed them, "He who listens to you listens to me; he who rejects you rejects me; but he who rejects me rejects the one who sent me" (Luke 10:16). In John 10, there are numerous references to the sheep hearing and recognizing the voice of the Good Shepherd. The voice of the Father commands believers to "listen to him" (Matt. 17:5). From these and other passages it is clear that listening to God is a critical discipline that is often developed through listening also to others whom He has sent. "He who has ears to hear, let him hear." (Luke 8:8b; 14:35b; Matt. 11:15; 13:9; Mark 4:9b)

> *"He who has ears to hear, let him hear."*

A second important coaching skill modeled by Jesus is the art of asking powerful questions. This is passing the ball so the person you are coaching can take a shot. Although Jesus frequently asked rhetorical questions, He also asked powerful questions in the context of teachable moments.[4] Perhaps Jesus paused, as a profound spiritual coach, between the powerful question series of Mark 8:17-19: "Why are you talking about having no bread? Do you still not see or understand? Are your hearts hardened? Do you have eyes but fail to see, and ears but fail to hear? And don't you remember? When I broke the five loaves for the five thousand, how many basketfuls of pieces did you pick up?" Any one of these serves as a powerful question in the context of an alongsider coaching relationship.

In both Mark 10:36 and 10:51, Jesus asked in two different settings, "What do you want me to do for you?" This could be perceived as God asking about one's desires, but in the context it is clearly Jesus, as a man, offering help in a way that captures an alongsider coaching moment. The disciples learned, through the modeling and coaching of Jesus, the meaning of servant leadership and the value of faith in the healing process. Good coaching includes offering help, "What can I do for you?" This is also recognizing that only Jesus can offer true help, but we can be an instrument. We can help by asking a powerful question and listening for God to do something wonderful. Sometimes you can offer a hand, because in doing so you might find opportunity for deeper coaching.

Other Biblical Models

Abram may have applied some coaching skills when he said to Lot, "Let's not have any quarreling between you and me, or between your herdsmen and mine, for we are brothers. Is not the whole land before you? Let's part company. If you go to the left, I'll go to the right; if you go to the right, I'll go to the left" (Gen. 13:8-9). Consider Abram's question, "Is not the whole land before you?" What a great question to ask as another person. What possibilities are ahead for you? What are the opportunities God might be putting in your path? What dreams might you dare to dream? After his question, Abram makes some "if" statements which empowered Lot to make a choice on his playing field of life.

Joseph also did some amazing coaching, in an upward fashion, with Pharaoh of Egypt. Even though Pharaoh was a superior with authority over him, Joseph coached up. When Pharaoh wanted an interpretation of his dreams, Joseph said, "I cannot do it" (Gen. 41:16a). A good alongsider coach is more interested in God leading people than feeding personal ego with expert answers. Alongsider coaching has in view the desire to help people hear from God. Joseph went on to say, "but God will give Pharaoh the answer he desires" (Gen.

41:16b). An alongsider coach prayerfully desires God to give people the answers they need.

> *An alongsider coach prayerfully desires God to give people the answers they need.*

There are also some elements of coaching that can be learned from the relationship of Joseph with his brothers (Gen. 41-50). When Joseph revealed himself to the brothers in Genesis chapter forty-five, he retold the story of how they had mistreated him and sold him into slavery to Egypt. However, he told the story from God's point of view. "But God sent me ahead of you to preserve for you a remnant on earth and to save your lives by a great deliverance." (Gen. 45:7) Good alongsider coaches retell stories with wisdom, painting a picture from God's perspective that fits the circumstances people find themselves facing.

There are many other biblical role models and heroes to be emulated by those who would like to serve as alongsider coaches. Abraham followed God's calling and took others with him on the journey of faith (Heb. 11:8-19; Gen. 12:4-5, 13:7-12). Moses seemed to have a coaching relationship with his brother Aaron (Exod. 4:28, 5:1, 7:7-9; Heb. 11:23-29; 1 Chron. 23:13). "Moses and Aaron are linked in Exodus 7:7-9. Moses was also a coach for Joshua (Exod. 24:13; Num. 11:26-30, 13:16, 27:18-23; Heb. 11:23-29).

Naomi was a coach for Ruth, helping her to make the journey from being a foreigner to a faithful follower (Ruth 1:8-18).

> *There was honesty, persistence, and directness in the words that encouraged Ruth to make a choice.*

There was honesty, persistence, and directness in the words that encouraged Ruth to make a choice.

Esther displayed the qualities of courage, commitment, and character to the inspiration of others (Est. 2:19-20, 4:15-17, 5:1-8). Because she understood human nature and relationships, she was able to take advantage of the circumstances and won the favor of the king and others. It could be argued that Mordecai (Esther's foster father) encouraged and coached her toward an intentional commitment to the call of God, *for such a time as this* (Est. 2:11, 3:2, 4:1, 4:15-17, 10:2-3). He was concerned enough to stay informed as to her welfare (2:11). He was observant, sitting at the gate watching and listening. Those are great coaching skills.

There are great examples of coaching qualities in the New Testament as well. Lydia was a worshiper of God who prayed with other people. She opened her home and others came to faith in Christ (Acts 16:12-15, 40). She was identified as "one of those listening" in Acts 16:14. In Acts 16:15, she was saying, in essence, "Get involved with my home life." She was responsive, hospitable, and persuasive.

Priscilla and Aquila were a team who made an impact, working hard as tent-makers, faithfully encouraging the saints by sharing their spiritual insights (Acts 18:18, 24-26; Rom. 16:3-5; 1 Cor. 16:19). They are always mentioned together in the Scriptures, serving as a model for team coaching.[5] They hung out with Paul, journeying with him to Syria. They are identified as risk taking, sacrificial, fellow workers in Romans 16:3-4. First Corinthians 16:19 identifies them as relationally warm, hosting a church in their home. They engaged in some spiritual coaching for Apollos, who then multiplied himself to influence others (Acts 18:24-26; 1 Cor. 16:12; Tit. 3:13).

If any of these saints were in the world today, it could be said that they would be great spiritual coaches.

A Cloud of Alongsider Witnesses

Many contemporary heroes of faith can be identified as models of alongsider coaching. "Therefore, since we are surrounded by such a great cloud of witnesses, let us throw off everything that hinders and the sin that so easily entangles, and let us run with perseverance the race marked out for us." (Heb. 12:1-2). Since the inception of the early church, examples abound of people who have walked as committed followers of Jesus and multiplied themselves in the discipling of other people around them.

On a "guys' weekend out," our little band of brothers headed up into the high country of the Trinity Alps of Northern California. It was a brutal, steep, six-mile hike. We carried loaded backpacks on a climb gaining 3,500 feet on a well marked trail which was worn by many hikers who had traveled that route over the years. As we walked the trail, I thought about the ascent to higher spiritual places with Jesus marked with a path left by the saints who have gone before us. Many are the people of faith who have made the quest, announcing their discovery of God as their victory, their shield, the one who guards the course. They have left signs and footprints that are helpful for our journey.

About half way up, we started walking in snow. Several times we lost the trail, because it was covered with a cold, white blanket. We encountered the need for wisdom, asking, "Which is the right way?" We always managed to get back on the main trail somehow, with God's help, but only after blazing a new and fresh pathway in getting back to the established trail. We arrived at the same destination as many others before, but didn't get there in exactly the same steps. At times we were doing something creative and new on the ascent.

That also happens on the path of life. Sometimes, the trail for us is hidden by the snowfalls of contemporary circumstances. The media, worldwide suffering, relational struggles, materialism, sin, the list is as long as the individual snowflakes which contribute to the snowy obstacles each of us encounter on the journey. The

Alongsider coaching helps to identify the path beneath the distractions.

next step is always one of faith, especially when the path is temporarily unclear. Often, alongsider coaching helps to identify the path beneath the distractions.

Jesus is the only way (John 14:6), and only He can lead us safely on this hike of faith. Yet, even through confusing terrain, He sometimes takes us on a quest full of fresh opportunities which require blazing a trail into new and uncharted places, with the blessing of bright scenery and a whole new perspective. Victory, new understanding, and wisdom at higher places come through trusting Him step by step as we walk together.

Whether this faith journey takes you through territory common to those who have gone before, or perhaps launches you into new places with a creative stride; whether placing your feet in the footsteps of past heroes of the faith or breaking new trails through the snowpack of our day, be encouraged to follow where He leads. Walk that journey with others alongside. That is a good, right, and guarded path, and it is one we need to travel with a band of others walking in alongsider, disciple-making relationships.

CHAPTER 3

THE LOVE FACTOR

*You can give without loving, but you cannot love
without giving. ~Amy Carmichael~*

Some religious guys came to Jesus one day and asked Him
to give them the bottom line. As they put it, "What is the
greatest commandment in the law?" (Matt. 22:36). Jesus put it
simply while expressing profound truth when He said, "Love
the Lord your God" (Matt. 22:37). If Jesus noted love for God
as the first and greatest commandment, it must be the first and
greatest alongsider coaching concern. To love God includes
loving what He loves. He loves
people. Alongsider coaching is
about loving God by loving people
enough to walk alongside them in relationships that help them
to become all they can be in Christ.

> *To love God includes
> loving what He loves.*

Love can be traced back to the beginning in the book
of Genesis. God had a close love relationship with the first
humans. Other relationships that unfolded in the book of
Genesis rose and fell on the scales of love. Love is a key
biblical foundation for a coaching relationship.

The people who have influenced me the most are those
who have walked alongside me in a relationship of trust
established in love. A former pastor and his wife walked with
us in preparing to go overseas. My father, as I grew into my
teen years, did less directive parenting and more coaching by
asking good questions, listening, sharing his life, and letting me
learn from mistakes. Walking alongside another person doesn't

require a degree in counseling or expertise in a profession. It calls for genuine love for God that moves your heart to love what He loves. God loves people, and so must we.

At the end of John's gospel, Jesus asked Peter, "Simon, son of John, do you love me more than these?" (John 21:15b). Then again He asked, "Simon son of John, do you love me?" (John 21:16). A third time Jesus asked him, "Simon son of John, do you love me?" (John 21:17a). Three times Jesus asked about Peter's love for Him. If you were asked this just once, how would you answer? What evidence would there be?

Intimacy with Christ Rooted in Love

The alongsider coaching relationship is one of love which flows from the heart of our Father God. The effective coach will help a coachee cultivate this love relationship through Bible study, prayer and worship, and other spiritual disciplines of the faith which encourage a walk in the fullness of the Holy Spirit of God (Gal. 5:24-25). The goal of alongsider coaching is becoming more like Jesus through a growing love for Him.

> *The goal of alongsider coaching is becoming more like Jesus through a growing love for Him.*

A core message of the Bible is the centrality of the person and work of Jesus Christ. Thus, a coaching relationship must be rooted in the cultivation of this love theology of the Christian life. The book of Colossians summarizes this topic with such grandeur, giving a beautiful image of the supremacy and centrality of Christ:

> For in Christ all the fullness of the Deity lives in bodily form, and in Christ you have been brought to fullness. He is the head over every power and authority. In him you were also circumcised with a circumcision not performed by human hands. Your sinful nature was

put off when you were circumcised by Christ, having been buried with him in baptism, in which you were also raised with him through your faith in the working of God, who raised him from the dead (Col. 2:9-12).

The only appropriate response to the centrality of Jesus is intimacy with Him, embracing Christ in all His fullness. Jesus profoundly said, "I am the vine, you are the branches. If a man remains in me and I in him, he will bear much fruit; apart from me you can do nothing" (John 15:5). There is a clear answer to the question of how much anyone can accomplish without Jesus: Nothing. We can do nothing at all of any eternal significance without Jesus Christ. An effective coach will keep Christ central in everything, and help the coachee to do the same, cultivating a heart relationship of intimacy with Jesus. Apart from the centrality of Christ and intimacy with Him, alongsider coaching would be a pointless exercise. It would simply be a meaningless walk.

> *An effective coach will keep Christ central in everything.*

An alongsider coach will instill in others the deep value of loving God by loving the people He loves. Loving God means loving the Church, the body of Christ. It means loving the lost and caring for the poor. It means acknowledging that God put talents, skills, and assets into each person that are to be called out and used wisely for His glory (Luke 16:1-15).

If you really love Jesus, you will not be able to contain it. Living water isn't to be kept in a reservoir, it is to well up unto eternal life and bring refreshment to thirsty people in our world. A slough overgrown with algae, weeds, and moss is not very inviting to a thirsty traveler. A freshwater spring-fed mountain stream is, especially close to the source. Let your love for Jesus flow with contagious refreshment.

The Biblical Mandate to Love Incarnationally

Continuing from the first portion of what is known as the greatest commandment, the gospel writer records, "And the second is like it: 'Love your neighbor as yourself.' All the Law and the Prophets hang on these two commandments" (Matt. 22:39-40). Love for God overflows into love for others, inspiring believers to engage Christ's mission to dwell among people and live incarnational lives. As Jesus took on bodily form and fulfilled the incarnation, His followers are invited to live in Him and for Him in such a way that they embody Christ in them, the hope of glory. That is contagious, and it can be powerfully expressed through alongsider relationships rooted in love.

What about the part of this passage which speaks of loving your neighbor as yourself? There is a biblical perspective here in regards to loving yourself. You could argue that the text is making the assumption you already do love yourself. That's true. For the most part. Much of the time. But not always. Sometimes people love themselves by hating themselves. Did you know it is possible to love hating yourself? Some people hate their neighbor because they hate themselves.

We need to love ourselves, but only through the grid of God's love for us. He delights in us, He loves us with an everlasting love. God wants us to have His love and share it; to receive it, return it, express it, and give it away. Alongsiding is a great context for that.

> *We need to love ourselves, but only through the grid of God's love for us.*

Just prior to the ascension, some of the final words of Jesus give us a compelling theology in regards to the critical value of engaging the mission of the Savior out of love:

> Then Jesus came to them and said, "All authority in heaven and on earth has been given to me. Therefore go and make disciples of all nations, baptizing them in

the name of the Father and of the Son and of the Holy Spirit, and teaching them to obey everything I have commanded you. And surely I am with you always, to the very end of the age" (Matt. 28:18-20).

This passage has become known as the "Great Commission," and it flows from the "Great Commandment" of Matthew 22:36-40. Great coaching keeps this great content clearly in view, and great churches result. The seeds for these thoughts were planted in the opening pages of the Bible. "Be fruitful and increase in number; fill the earth and subdue it." (Gen. 1:28b) The main thrust of those words were to instill purpose into those first humans for populating the earth. For all of us, it includes participating with God in reproducing children of God (John 3). It also means investing in other people in our families, neighborhoods, and communities. For some of us, this means establishing long-term relationships in a cross-cultural setting. It might mean answering the call to go to a place that is foreign (Gen. 12:1). It is not a theological stretch to connect the command to be fruitful with His invitation to join Him in building an abundant kingdom under the kingship of Jesus Christ. God gives His people work to do; that work should be embraced out of love; and alongsider coaching is an important way to disciple people and equip Jesus' followers for the work of God in and through them.

Furthermore, God empowers His people to accomplish whatever He calls them to do. "But you will receive power when the Holy Spirit comes on you; and you will be my witnesses in Jerusalem, and in all Judea and Samaria, and to the ends of the earth." (Acts 1:8) Believers are invited to embrace Christ and engage His mission; He is with them always; He empowers them for it; and spiritual coaches have

> *God empowers His people to accomplish whatever He calls them to do.*

the profound opportunity to be used to accomplish it as they tap into the spring of God's love and let it flow.

Interdependent Love

I really like the city of Philadelphia, a place filled with the history of our independence as a nation. It is the city of independence. Independence rings of personal rights and responsibilities held in high esteem. These values work best if kept in balance by interdependence. A wonderful paradox is discovered there—interdependent independence.

The journey of faith is one of interdependence. Walking alongside other people in relational interdependence out of love for God and for each other is something beautiful. Alongsider coaching cultivates interdependence rooted in love. Alongsider coaching is about love for God and His story, a fountainhead of love that flows like living water toward interdependent communities of faith.

> *Alongsider coaching cultivates interdependence rooted in love.*

Alongsider coaching involves relational interdependence. People need others to walk alongside—not ahead, not behind, not over top of, but alongside. In western culture, an independent mindset can create a path that ends with people walking alone. In many cultures, alongsiding is more natural because of the "we" social identity set in contrast with the "me" independent identity. People need others to walk with, people who will communicate, "I'm on your side." People need people who will model what it looks like to be on the same team, people who will live life with others.

While visiting some friends in Philadelphia, we spent some time with a pastor and his wife in their home. We discovered that the wife had an amazing ability to spin wool by hand. Watching her demonstrate the skill with which she was able to spin the wheel with her foot and feed raw wool into the machine was intriguing. Twisting the fibers into a thread of yarn makes it possible to knit warm blankets or coats of many colors. We had a great discussion about what it's like to follow Christ, allowing Him to weave together something beautiful in a world that seems to be spiraling downward around us.

Be it tornadoes and floods or job security and suffering, there are days when the circumstances around us seem like a whirlwind. Many people we know are just trying to keep their heads above water in storms they hope will go away. Much is out of our hands and over our heads, yet God is within our reach in a world full of uncertainties.

On the cross, Jesus wore a garment that was seamless, woven in one piece. They didn't tear it. Perhaps they couldn't rip the garment, like the fulfilled prophecy that none of His bones were broken. Consider the passage:

When the soldiers crucified Jesus, they took his clothes, dividing them into four shares, one for each of them, with the undergarment remaining. This garment was seamless, woven in one piece from top to bottom. "Let's not tear it," they said to one another. "Let's decide by lot who will get it." (John 19:23-24)

In Christ, through an intimate relationship with Jesus, "We are hard pressed on every side, but not crushed; perplexed, but not in despair; persecuted, but not abandoned; struck down, but not destroyed" (2 Cor. 4:8-10). As we clothe ourselves in Christ, God works everything to the good, creating a beautiful garment that will endure the spin of our world, "...to make known among the Gentiles the glorious riches of this mystery, which is Christ in you, the hope of glory" (Col. 1:27).

Even with all the spin and confusion, I believe deeply that God can work things to the good for those who love Him (Rom. 8:28). We can embrace a hope and a future in a relationship with Christ. He can weave something beautiful out of our lives, even in the most out-of-control situations spinning around us. Alongsider coaches who root their relationships in love are often God's tools to help people discover a no spin zone.

Freedom from Independence

On a drive through Nevada on our way to Montana, my family and I encountered an interesting sign. It was one of those big green exit signs, announcing the exit for "Independence Valley." Beneath it was further information, announcing, "No services. Prison Area. Hitchhiking Prohibited." What a contrast, a prison in Independence Valley! Independence, freedom from the control and influence of others, was contrasted with the regulating guards and prohibitive walls. A great discussion in our family flowed from that scene. Could the unrestrained exercise of our own independence actually become a form of imprisonment? Is it possible to become a prisoner of your own pursuit of independence, constrained by the category by which we define it? If we are left to invent ourselves, we end up in the bondage of self, captives of that which we pursue for selfish independence. Independence freely sought doubles back for a handshake with the imprisonment of an empty destination. What the world offers for independence can be costly. The self-imposed jail of self-determination is a dangerous place.

There is a better alternative, being in dependence on Christ and His Word. That is the self-denial of your own rights in order to move in the right direction. Love is not self-seeking (1 Cor. 13:5). Every person needs an alongsider to help them really break free from independence and move toward interdependence growing out of dependence on God alone.

Jonathan and David

Consider the example of Jonathan serving as a coach for David (1 Sam. 18-23). Jonathan was the firstborn son of Saul, rightful heir of the throne, but he knew David was chosen by God, anointed to become the king. They made a covenant together, promises rooted in love. "And Jonathan made a covenant with David because he loved him as himself." (1 Sam. 18:3). Their relationship is a great example of alongsider coaching.

What did love look like for Jonathan and David? One expression was loyalty. In 1 Samuel 18:4, Jonathan extended to David gifts of royal clothing and instruments of war. This is symbolic of bonding, a display of face to face loyalty. Jonathan knew that David would one day be king, and he extended honor to him. It is a display of loyal commitment to help David prepare for his kingship. This loyalty unfolds again later. "But show me unfailing kindness like that of the Lord." (1 Sam. 20:14-15) The Hebrew word for unfailing kindness is *hesed*, meaning love and loyalty, two essential aspects of a covenant relationship bound up in one Old Testament word.[6] Perhaps the greatest kind of loyalty is found in Jonathan's example, loyalty out of love.

David and Jonathan also exemplified that their covenant was about how love and loyalty is demonstrated in both protection and confrontation. In Jonathan's coaching relationship with David, this is magnified as being even more important than blood family bonds. His love for David extended beyond any loyalties he felt toward King Saul, his father. This protecting, guarding another person's "back," is an important quality of an alongsider coach.

> *Love and loyalty is demonstrated in both protection and confrontation.*

Often, protective coaching means keeping secrets and maintaining confidence. In 1 Samuel 20, Jonathan checked things out in confidence, keeping a secret as to where David was. David was out hiding on the south side of a big stone. Sometimes the best service we can offer is to keep confidence with people as they wait in the field, sitting at the stone altar, allowing God our Rock to bring healing and refining. Protecting can also mean covering for people whom we are coaching. It means speaking on their behalf, as Jonathan did for David: "Jonathan spoke well of David to Saul his father" (1 Sam. 19:4a).

In chapter nineteen, Jonathan gave warnings of impending danger. Sometimes loving loyalty in a coaching relationship is about warnings. "Stay away from that." "Avoid that person." This kind of protective coaching involves confrontation. Love is kind, but love also confronts.

Love is kind, but love also confronts.

Commitment, rooted in love, is also a key part of coaching. In 1 Samuel 20:4, Jonathan said something every follower of Jesus should hear at some point: "Whatever you want me to do, I'll do for you." That is commitment. Love and loyalty are about commitment. Although the people we are coaching must be the ones who do the work, they need to know that someone is there for them. David went out into the field with the assurance that Jonathan was advocating on his behalf. Coaches encourage by commitment to be there and be available, whatever it takes.

Alongsider coaching culminates in sending. We need to love people enough to launch them forward beyond ourselves. In 1 Samuel 20:42, David got up from the south side of the stone and bowed down before Jonathan three times, with his face to the ground, indicating honor to a superior. They wept together, David the most, but there was a sharing in common bonds of emotion. Jonathan said to David, "Go in peace." This was something generally

Alongsider coaching culminates in sending.

said by a superior, firming up the fact that Jonathan all along had been a coach to David. At the same time, however, Jonathan used the emphatic "we" as a reminder of the covenant relationship between two friends. The friendship launched David forward. "Then David left, and Jonathan went back to town." (1 Sam. 20:42) In essence, David was sent forth into the next phase of his development. Jonathan went back to where he was.

It wasn't that they never met again. In chapter twenty-three, with David in the desert, knowing that Saul was out to kill him, Jonathan went to David and "helped him find strength in God" (1 Sam. 23:18). He said to David, "Don't be afraid." That is a powerful coaching encouragement. They remembered and renewed their covenant. The alongsider coach stepped into the picture once again, bringing strength and encouragement at a critical moment on the battlefield of life.

In the example of Jonathan the coach, it is clear that coaching is about long-term impact, a life-changing investment during a period of time. By 2 Samuel 9, much had happened. There had been many battles, with both defeat and victory. Saul and Jonathan are now dead, killed in war. The text finds David remembering Jonathan. He missed the friendship and remembered their covenant. He recalled the tremendous coaching impact Jonathan had on him.

The covenant between Jonathan and David was a warrior love. I sat next to a retired policeman once, on a flight to San Francisco. He talked about some very close friends who were U.S. Marines. He spoke of the bonds between Marines who have been in battle together, and how they have a deep connection seldom experienced by civilians. There is a deep trust which develops when you have covered each other's backs, taken fire together, been injured and carried by a team, and seen the worst that the enemy can throw at you.

Paul and Timothy had that kind of bond as soldiers of Christ. "Suffer hardship with me, as a good soldier of Christ Jesus. No soldier in active service entangles himself in the affairs of everyday life, so that he may please the one who enlisted him as a soldier." (2 Tim. 2:3-4) We battle darkness with weapons not of this world (2 Cor. 10:3-5). Who are your brothers, sisters, and fellow soldiers in the fellowship of battle? What are you doing that invades the turf of the enemy and reaches out to people? Marching alongside together out of love for God brings victory.

CHAPTER 4

ACTIVE LISTENING

Therefore consider carefully how you listen.
~Luke 8:18a~

Big game hunting is a very exciting sport for many people out west. Fall is the season of year when the bull elk are bugling (a musical call they sing out in challenge to other bulls). My eldest son and I were alongside hunting several miles into the Wind River wilderness area of Wyoming, and saw two cow elk. Then we heard the bugle of a bull, beautiful music to our ears. He sounded big. We spent the next hour sneaking through the mountain timber and bugling the song of the elk with our imitation call, repeatedly hearing his melodic response. We would bugle and then he would answer. We were getting closer to him, and he was responding to the challenge. The excitement was building. Nearing the spot where we heard his last bugle, we prepared ourselves and got ready to harvest a large bull elk. We stooped behind some bushes and readied our archery equipment. We knew he was nearly in sight. Our hearts were pounding with the excitement and anticipation of that moment when we would see his magnificent antlers.

The moment was derailed. We were surprised to hear the voice of humans, then we saw them. We suddenly realized that we had been hunting hunters who were also imitating the voice of the elk. We felt a bit foolish. Following the hunter's code, we avoided eye contact and drifted back into the woods like nothing happened. The crunch of time and energy wasted left us empty handed, feeling tricked and robbed. The excitement of potential success turned to the discouragement of having run in the wrong race after the wrong prize.

How many times have I done that in life, chasing after the wrong voice, following the wrong song, hunting for the wrong treasures, seeking after the counterfeits of life that crushed the excitement when reality struck? Alongsider coaching is about healthy listening, to God first. It is also about listening well to the people we are seeking to coach, helping them to hear God's voice first and foremost. There are many distracting voices, and the passion of the alongsider is to tune into God and not waste time chasing the many distractions of our day. Jesus gives a wonderful promise in this regard, "My sheep hear my voice, and I know them, and they follow me" (John 10:27).

One of the important skills for alongside coaching is active listening. Listening is an ability that can be developed. Good listening often flows from self-discipline and keeping the needs of the coachee as the priority. Jesus modeled active listening. He listened first and foremost to the Father, but also actively listened to the people around Him. Listening was a key spiritual discipline that He modeled and taught (Matt. 13:18; 15:10; 17:5; 18:16-17; 21:33; Mark 4:3; 7:14; 9:44; John 10:1-27). Listening is a gift.

> *Jesus modeled active listening.*

Fallen Listening

In the Garden of Eden, Adam and Eve walked in an active, engaging relationship with God. You can be certain that good listening was happening in their love for each other. Using a sanctified imagination, you can picture Adam listening to God, Eve conversing with God, and Adam and Eve communicating effectively with each other in God's presence. Life was good.

However, Genesis chapter three happened. Listening was sidetracked and poor choices were made. Eve started listening to Satan rather than staying tuned in to God. But we can't leave Adam off the hook. What was he up to? What was he thinking? What if he had been tuned in to the conversation rather than sitting there writing on fig leaves or doing e-mail or whatever he was distracted with? The Scripture says that he was there, but he wasn't really there. He wasn't really listening.

You see, there are two kinds of listening, active listening and passive listening. Passive listening is like the opposite of talking. It means our lips aren't moving but our minds are, often with thoughts in another place. Adam was passive listening. Active listening is redemptive, purposeful, and fruitful. Passive listening and disobedience brought a curse into the created order, sabotaging our ability to really hear. Thankfully, God is good at opening ears.

> *There are two kinds of listening, active listening and passive listening.*

As a young driver, my father helped me with the purchase of my first car. It was a push button Dodge Dart. It was not a new car, in fact it burned oil. Sometimes I forgot to check the oil. My dad was good about reminding me, and I heard his reminders but I failed to listen well. Passive listening led to burning up the engine one day. It was an expensive lesson about the importance of active listening that tunes us in to our heavenly Father and to other people, both as we are coaching and as we are being coached.

Redeemed Listening

Active listening takes energy and intentionality. Active listening is listening without an agenda. Active listening includes listening with a third ear to the Holy Spirit, asking questions like, "What is God doing, what is He saying?" "Where are His fingerprints?" Active listening will help you to help people to experience Spirit-led discovery.

It is easy to be a passive listener, simply looking at the other person, sitting quietly and nodding occasionally while the mind is on the beach in Hawaii. In active listening, the coach works to draw out the speaker's meaning. That includes providing nonjudgmental verbal feedback to check your understanding of what the coachee is saying. That means probing and asking questions so that the focus is not simply on what you think of the other person's message, but on what the person is really saying and what the person really means. Reaching that place is only possible through intentional, engaged, active listening.

The effective coach also learns to be free from the addiction of telling. This means recovering from the tendency all of us have of constantly talking and giving advice, developing the capacity to really listen.[7] I was listening to an interview on the radio recently with a man who had just turned eighty-eight. The interviewer asked the man, "What is the most important thing you have learned after eighty-eight years?" I turned up the volume about then, wanting to hear what he had to say. The seasoned gentleman responded, "Don't give out so much advice."

> *The effective coach learns to be free from the addiction of telling.*

It's not that giving advice is always bad, especially if people are really asking for it and especially if it includes sharing mistakes we have made and learned from. It is good if others can learn from our blunders, and that kind of advice can stick. Somebody told me once that the early bird gets the worm, but the second mouse usually gets the cheese. Timely advice can help others avoid neck-breaking traps. However, telling and giving advice must be carefully and strategically timed with wisdom and discernment.

Listen Physically

By God's enabling and with self-discipline, you can learn to listen with all of your senses engaged. You can listen physically. That means good eye contact, which is essential. Staring doesn't help, but strategic eye connection is powerful. It is wise to be aware of another person's eyes as you listen, listening and observing what they are saying.

My first childhood memory was of being very sick, with a high fever. I recall waking up in the middle of the night, feeling the fever and the confused fear that it brings. My mother and father were holding me over the sink, wetting me down to bring the fever under control. What I remember most vividly was looking into my father's eyes. They were eyes of compassion, and yet eyes marked by a calm peace that brought tremendous comfort to me as a child. That memory has often informed my passions for coaching people, looking them in the eye in a way that communicates compassion and sends the message that things are going to be okay. Your eyes engaging another person can be, in a potent way, the Heavenly Father's eyes to bring hope and build peace.

To listen physically means avoiding distracting activities like tapping your foot or closed postures like folded arms. People can tell when you aren't really interested in a conversation. Alongsider coaches generate an attitude of interest by listening with engaged eye contact, with postures and expressions that

> *Alongsider coaches generate an attitude of interest.*

express empathy and concern. This is often demonstrated through an open posture which communicates interest. You might try leaning in slightly, expressing a desire to focus on what is being shared.

Sometimes our struggle to listen well shows up with those we love the most, at least that is the case with me. When my wife is talking and processing with me, it is far too easy to continue checking texts or e-mail messages, read the newspaper, or fade in and out as my mind wanders. That is never good for a relationship. Good listening is expressed with our bodies and an awareness of their eyes, your eyes, and God's.

The best example I witnessed of this kind of listening was when I was teaching in a Christian school in Montana. I will never forget observing a student as he dropped in with a problem he needed to talk about with the principal, who was a very busy man. The administrator's work load could be quickly discerned by the amount of paperwork piled up on his desk. As the student began to talk, it was obvious that the caring leader was consumed by the tasks before him, but he did something amazing in order to adjust and give his full attention to the needy student. With one broad sweep of his arm he pushed everything off his desk. The crashing noise accented his honest desire to focus all energy on that student. It was a dramatic and loud expression of the intention with which he desired to listen.

He leaned across the desk with full, engaging eye contact. It was a great example of redemptive listening. That student received a wonderful gift of listening with a leader who cared. I believe God enjoyed watching that scene of good alongsider coaching.

Listening physically also means listening environmentally. That means awareness of what is happening around you and removing, if possible, those distractions that could deter effective listening. Peaceful background music could be strategic. I've been in homes where the TV was so loud that an effective coaching conversation was next to impossible. Listening physically means minimizing interruptions and maximizing safety and confidentiality with attention to body

For some of us, the opposite of talking is waiting to talk.

language and posture. The recipient of such focused listening is blessed.

Listen Relationally and Emotionally

For some of us, the opposite of talking is waiting to talk. Many of us think that not speaking when someone is talking is the same as listening. We must understand that hearing the words people are speaking is only the beginning of active listening. An effective coach will try to hear the fears and anxieties behind the talking. An effective coach will tune into the unspoken signals of intentions and aspirations. Listening helps you gain insights and come to a deeper place of understanding of the fingerprints of God in a person's life. People also are encouraged and inspired when they discern that we are genuinely interested and that we care.

Listening relationally means listening first to what God is up to. What is the Holy Spirit saying and doing? Good coaching is always with the awareness of God's presence and His voice speaking into the relationship and the situation. This kind of listening, rooted in prayer, helps the coach discern where God is working in the coachee's life.

Intimate relationship with God flows into authentic relationships with people you are coaching. The coach must learn to prayerfully place his or her own problems on hold to give full attention to the person being coached. That means learning to wait patiently through periods of silence or tears. Good listening is a gift that builds relationship.

> *Good listening is a gift that builds relationship.*

It is important for an alongsider coach to hear the feeling of the verbal message, taking note of what is being said between the lines. That means tuning in to hear what they are "not" saying. Are any details being left out because of emotional trauma? Do the person's expressions and emotions match the words being said? My wife and I encountered a person not long ago who started telling a story about something that happened in her life, something that was heart wrenching and painful. Her expressions and emotions didn't match the pain that would be expected in the telling of such an agonizing story. She admitted later that she didn't completely trust us yet, and she was probing to see what our reaction would be. Would we give up on her? Would we judge her? Would we overreact with shocking disbelief? Listening relationally and emotionally helped us to earn her trust.

Probing questions are helpful for becoming a better emotional listener. It is good to go deeper and clarify the issues for greater understanding. It is helpful to learn the art of reflective listening and avoid reflexive listening. In other words, carefully consider the deeper message (reflective listening) and avoid the tendency to simply wait for your chance to say something in response (reflexive listening).[8]

Although it might feel awkward until practiced, echoing back what another person has said can be strategic in opening a door for deeper conversations. Active listening to discover the meaning beneath the message and between the lines is good alongsider coaching.

The Art of Silence

I'm a deep thinker. As a result, I need to actively jettison my own mental journey that could take me on rabbit trails or cause me to be thinking about what I'm going to say next. In that regard, good listening will include moments of silence. I'm learning to be ok with that, intentionally turning off my mind and my agenda in order to really listen, then letting my thoughts formulate a question or comment and be ok if it takes silence to accomplish it. Silence is not a bad thing.

Good listening often means getting used to silence, especially in the midst of emotional moments. Silence should never be feared. Amazing things can happen in moments

Silence should never be feared.

of silence. Most of us try to fill silent spots in a conversation too quickly. As a teacher, one of my supervising principals once coached me with an encouraging challenge. He said I was very good at asking questions to solicit classroom discussion. He encouraged me by saying that I might try getting comfortable with silence in order to wait for students to answer rather than answering my own questions because of impatience with non-immediate response or discomfort with the quiet time it might take to get there. Silence can be golden.

True listening means there will be moments of silence. Silence is sometimes perceived as unendurable. Silence makes us nervous and uncomfortable. We often have unwarranted fears that silence may be interpreted as low self-esteem or questionable intelligence. We feel like we are expected to impress others with witty comments and wise observations that speak to the issue on the spot. Many of us feel, sometimes subconsciously, that silence is a form of nonparticipation that communicates a lack of interest or the notion that we simply don't have anything more to say.[9] Get comfortable with silence. Furthermore, be aware that emotionally charged subjects may require more silent moments.

Learning how to embrace silence starts with our prayer life. I heard a story once that in the eighteenth century, a pastor noticed a peasant sitting in the sanctuary of the church, but it

> *Learning how to embrace silence starts with our prayer life.*

was a rather strange scene. The peasant was just sitting there in the pew, not even seeming to be praying. Yet, he was happy just being there. The pastor approached him and asked the peasant what he was doing there for such a long time. The man replied, "I look at Him, He looks at me, and we are happy together." Try sitting before God in silence. It can build relationship with the Father. Prayer is opportunity to let God coach us, and I don't ever want to miss His quiet voice by doing all the talking.

If a relationship is good, trust has been earned, active listening is being practiced, and love is assured, silence can take a friendship deeper. Somebody told me once that they could recognize a good friend by the ability to sit together in a car without feeling uncomfortable about neither of them talking. Try it. Shhhhh……

Focused Listening

Good listening also means learning how to focus the ears when distracting sound waves compete. Great music can draw the heart away from current realities. Other conversations can derail the direction of the moment. Noise pollution can be to the detriment of good quality listening. The key word would be, "focus."

Camping memories have been treasures for our family. One of those adventures unfolded in the Daniel Boone National Forest of Kentucky. After purchasing a primitive camping permit, we found an ideal spot next to a clear stream with several trickling waterfalls. The campfire sparked a time of sharing stories. The sunset inspired a simple enjoyment of the silence. Not long after the light was fading, we headed for our bedrolls. We decided to forget the tent and stretch out under the stars, although we couldn't see many of them with the thick canopy of hardwood trees. The few stars in view were outshined by the full moon radiantly ruling the night.

The rolling shelf above the stream was a beautiful place to rest, but we faced the challenge of falling asleep as nonresidents in a noisy habitat. The crickets, bugs, and tree frogs (among other creatures I'm sure) were quite vocal with their various sounds. We thought at first that the forest inhabitants were singing a lullaby just for us, but it became an orchestra with too many hyper conductors. Their failure to change keys or tones grew into a major annoyance. It was a noisy highway, a dripping faucet, a crowded room of talkative people, a busy downtown intersection in the big city, the rhythmic tick of an old clock. It became an irritating sleep-robber, like the many competing voices that keep our minds busy and distract us from peace.

In the midst of all that noise, the freshwater stream nearby trickled ever so peacefully. Once our ears learned to focus on the persuading peace in the flow of the freshwater stream, our hearts moved toward rest. The quiet trickle won a peaceful victory, complete with a reflection of the confident moon over a multitude of stars. The natural sound of the water moving near our heads brought rest to our hearts. There was beautiful music in that river of life. The competing voices were still there, but they no longer ruled the night. God's peace reigned over the noisy darkness, another treasure in our bank of memories.

"For the Lamb at the center of the throne will be their shepherd; he will lead them to springs of living water. And God will wipe away every tear from their eyes." (Rev. 7:17) Those are words worth listening to with the focus of active listening. The alongsider coach can learn to be a powerful listener by learning to focus on His voice through His Word.

CHAPTER 5

THE POWER OF A GOOD QUESTION

What are you discussing together as you walk along?
~Luke 24:38~

Jesus asked incredibly powerful questions. Some of His questions might have seemed irritating, but they were powerful. Consider the scene in John 21:5 where He called out to the disciples with the question, "Friends, haven't you any fish?" This was after His death and resurrection, and they had gone back to fishing. They didn't know who was interrupting them from the shore, and as seasoned fishermen it might have seemed like a very irritating question. I don't know that I would have the courage to ask professional fishermen, hard working, rough looking men, a question revealing their lack of success. The question coming from Jesus, however, was powerful in setting the scene for the miracle of an overwhelming catch.

Jesus went on to say, "Throw your net on the right side of the boat and you will find some" (John 21:6). Once they postured themselves on the right side, they caught so many fish that their mental desktops came out of sleep mode. They recognized their Lord. Jesus hit the right key with a powerful question, and they caught something more profound than a bunch of fish.

An effective spiritual coach will follow in those footsteps, asking a question to set the stage for God to reveal something.

Questions are powerful when they position people for Spirit-
led, God-initiated discovery. I
served with a great Sunday
school teacher once who really
understood this. His practice
was to study the Scripture and develop a lesson plan, but then
he would go back and replace comments with questions. He
facilitated God-initiated discovery through discussion rather
than using only lecture. He understood the power of questions.

> *Questions are powerful when they position people for Spirit-led, God-initiated discovery.*

Powerful Questions for Spirit-Led Discovery

Asking strategic questions is a tremendous tool for spiritual
alongsider coaching. Consider this illustrative passage which
contains another powerful question:

> When Jesus looked up and saw a great crowd
> coming toward him, he said to Philip, "Where shall
> we buy bread for these people to eat?" He asked this
> only to test him, for he already had in mind what he
> was going to do. Philip answered him, "Eight months'
> wages would not buy enough bread for each one to
> have a bite!" Another of his disciples, Andrew, Simon
> Peter's brother, spoke up, "Here is a boy with five small
> barley loaves and two small fish, but how far will they
> go among so many?" Jesus said, "Have the people sit
> down." There was plenty of grass in that place, and
> the men sat down, about five thousand of them. Jesus
> then took the loaves, gave thanks, and distributed to
> those who were seated as much as they wanted. He did
> the same with the fish. When they had all had enough
> to eat, he said to his disciples, "Gather the pieces that
> are left over. Let nothing be wasted." So they gathered
> them and filled twelve baskets with the pieces of the
> five barley loaves left over by those who had eaten.
> After the people saw the miraculous sign that Jesus did,

they began to say, "Surely this is the Prophet who is to come into the world." Jesus, knowing that they intended to come and make him king by force, withdrew again to a mountain by himself (John 6:5-15).

In the context of life and ministry, seizing a teachable moment, Jesus asked a strategically loaded question in this passage, "Where shall we buy bread for these people to eat?" The question was powerful because, first of all, it was rooted in relationship. Note the inclusive "we" within the asking.

> *"Where shall we buy bread for these people to eat?"*

This "where" question of Jesus in John chapter six also builds expectation, which makes it powerful. "Where shall we buy bread for these people to eat?" (John 6:5b). Don't miss the direction and purpose in the "shall" of the question. The question is loaded with intentionality. Effective coaches build expectation and hope. A good coach equips in a way that builds expectancy and faith.

The question is also powerfully simple in its connection with a felt need. Everyone was hungry. Using a question to acknowledge a need of the moment builds relationship. It is of great strategic value to keep the coaching relationship organic and relational, always ready to adjust to the learning needs and life felt needs of the people we walk alongside. When a person is hungry for something in their life, an attentive coach can seize the opportunity to help position them to receive from God.

This question in John chapter six is also powerful because it shifts the responsibility to the disciples. That's what Jesus did, at least initially. Effective coaching does that, encouraging the coachee to be engaged in the work at hand. As Robert Logan explains in his book, *Coaching 101*, "The person being coached does the work."[10] That work can be initiated with a powerful question. Although an encouraging nudge is sometimes necessary, a well placed question can plant the responsibility in the good soil of a hungry person you are walking with.

There is another reason that Jesus' question is powerful; it is short and uncomplicated. His question is simple and to the point, yet sets in motion the learning of some profound truths. If a question is too long, the power gets lost by the resistance and friction between the beginning of the question to the final word. If a question is too complicated, the profound simplicity of the moment can be lost.

Jesus' question also helped the disciples discover all the resources within their reach. He already had in mind what He was going to do. In alongsiding, the coach often knows what needs to be done, but in the asking of a question the coach can solicit participation and involvement leading to a transformational experience. It is a wonderful blessing when the asking of a question nudges people into a place of hearing from God and not just from their coaches. Powerful things can happen when the stage is set with a question.

> *Powerful things can happen when the stage is set with a question.*

I saw a picture once of a man pulling a wagon with square wheels on the axles. You could see the burden in his facial expression. He was sweating hard, working laboriously. He probably had a severe headache from the bouncing of a craft designed more for parking on a hill than traveling on a path. Careful analysis of the picture revealed that inside the wagon was a load of round wheels. He was carrying what was necessary for efficient travel, but failed to see the resources.

Sometimes, coaching involves helping others to experience Spirit-led discovery of the provisions God has already made available even though they might be out of sight. That's where faith comes in, and alongsider coaching is a shared walk of faith with the potential to open a person's eyes to the resources

God has already supplied. The richest resources often reside in the person being coached, or within their reach, and alongsider coaches help people to see what God has already put in place.

Notice also that Jesus used an open-ended question in John chapter six. It could not be answered by a simple "yes" or "no." He could have asked, "Do we have any food?" Instead, He asked a question that set the stage and opened the way for a great miracle. It is most effective to ask open-ended questions whenever possible. This means keying in on the use of certain words such as "what" or "how." Statements that begin with verbs like "tell," "describe," and "explain" serve as good starting points for further questions.

> *It is most effective to ask open-ended questions whenever possible.*

As you may already be surmising, powerful questions are most potent when they are in tandem with active listening. In line with active listening, a good question can echo understanding of what has been said and take the conversation to a deeper level.

This story of multiplied bread sparked by a powerful question is a wonderful example of alongsider coaching. Jesus modeled active listening to discern the needs, asked a strategic question to initiate personal engagement and responsibility, and then asked the Father to multiply transformation and growth in the people nearby. Only after Jesus allowed them to unpack the resources within their reach, by asking a powerful question, did He step in with a miracle of multiplication.

Don't miss one last coaching principle. The passage in John six tells us that Jesus then withdrew to a mountain by Himself. I'm certain that His primary objective was alone time with the Father, but perhaps He also prayed for the disciples on the fields of ministry. It is strategic to pray for those we are coaching. Prayer can enlighten the best questions to ask.

Consider John chapter one, where Jesus called forth disciples. At one point (v. 38), He turned to those following and asked a powerful question, "What do you want?" In some versions it is translated, "What are you seeking?" Have you ever asked another person that question? Have you ever been asked by an alongsider, "Where do you want to be, where do you want to go, what do you want to do?" Helping a person realize where they are in their passions, desires, and dreams is powerful.

Jesus also asked two great questions in Mark 8:27-29, "Who do people say I am?" The disciples responded, "Some say John the Baptist; others say Elijah; and still others, one of the prophets." Then Jesus asked a follow-up question, "But what about you? Who do you say I am?" Every person, every generation, every culture needs to ask this question and coach others in the unpacking of the answers.

Wouldn't it be remarkable if every person making a decision to follow Jesus had a coach who walked alongside to help them be fully discipled? Wouldn't it be powerful if every partner in the gospel were able to start and finish well because of the relational investment of spiritual coaching? How strategic it would be for every teenager to have an alongsider coach to help them in their pursuit of God and His will. Life is full of coaching opportunities just waiting to happen. A coach comes alongside, in cooperation with the Holy Spirit, to encourage a person in the discovery of God's purposes on purpose using the tools of active listening and powerful questions.

Seven Questions From God

In Genesis chapters three and four, there are seven powerful questions from God. When the first man and woman took the

> *"Where are you?"*
> *(Gen. 3:9b)*

path of disobedience in Genesis chapter 3, the scene in the paradise of Eden provides great insight. As God was walking in the garden in the cool of the day, Adam and Eve hid from Him among the trees (Gen. 3:8). God asked a commanding question, "Where are you?" (Gen. 3:9b). It's not like God needed to find out where they were. He knew their exact location on His global positioning system. The question was designed for Adam and Eve to experience God-initiated discovery. The question is one that commands honesty. The question is, "Where are you, really?" It's not a question that can be answered with information about where you would like to be. It is not about where you'd like other people to think you are or where others really do think you are, but it is a question about where you are—really. I can't imagine a more powerful question. It is probably the best place to start in an alongsider coaching relationship. Where are you?

A second question comes in verse 11, "Who told you that you were naked? Have you eaten from the tree that I commanded you not to eat from?" In other words, who are you listening to and what are you feeding on? Alongsider coaching can help people to avoid the counsel of those who may not be following Jesus and are lacking in true wisdom (Ps. 1). Coaching can help people consider the source of the voices they are listening to. This kind of question can help to further clarify where people are and how they got there.

> *Coaching can help people consider the source of the voices they are listening to.*

The context of the questions in Genesis three and four is sin and judgment. However, we can see these inquiries through the lens of the new covenant in Christ, not with judgment or condemnation but with grace, mercy, and love.

The next question in these early pages of Scripture appears twice, one in regards to Adam and Eve and later again with Cain. "What is this you have done?" (Gen. 3:13, 4:10). The context makes this about rebellion and sin. For Adam and Eve, it was about the act of rebellion and disobedience. For Cain, it was a downward spiral of jealousy, anger, and hatred that led to murder. This question has the potential to set the stage for forgiveness and deliverance from bitterness. Similar questions might serve us well, like, "What have you done to get you where you are?" Or, "What have you done to get beyond where you are?"

Then God asked, "Why are you angry?" (Gen. 4:6). Questions like that can be powerful. Why is your face downcast? What is discouraging you? What is frustrating you? What sin is making you angry? Do you ever get mad at the sin in our world that impacts others? Do you ever get irritated at the sin in your own life?

It is good to keep in mind the importance of "tone" when asking questions like these. An inquisitive and nonjudgmental tone is vital to good coaching, and is received much better than an accusatory, sarcastic, or condescending manner that comes across as interrogation rather than alongsider coaching.

> *An inquisitive and nonjudgmental tone is vital to good coaching,*

In this regard, it is smart to avoid beginning a question with "why" because it can be perceived in the wrong light. God asked Cain a "why" question, but we need to be cautious with that one. Asking questions that begin with "why" can be a relational inhibitor. Often, questions beginning with "why" sound judgmental and loaded with potential accusation. Furthermore, people may not know why.

That being said, it would be good to note that Jesus asked some "why" questions. He asked more non-why questions, but one comes to mind. "Why are you troubled, and why do doubts rise in your minds?" (Luke 24:38). In the context, the question seems rhetorical and carries the tone of teaching the disciples to have peace, to trust in the powerful truth of His resurrection, to see Him for who He is. He wasn't judging their behavior or their choices, but He was setting the stage for discovery.

Back to the flow of Genesis, God then asked a penetrating question. It was like a double edged sword. "If you do what is right, will you not be accepted?" (Gen. 4:7). Doing what is right means doing it for God, seeking Him first and His righteousness. That means fearing God and not man, being accepted by God above all else. Everyone needs the acceptance of God which opens the door for relationship with Him. That means repentance, turning away from the wrong and getting re-centered on the right. The New Testament brings the other edge, that apart from Christ we can do nothing (John 15:4-5). In Christ is our hope of glory. So, for the alongsider coach, any question that helps people to see the righteous choices for God's pleasure rooted in Christ is a powerful question.

Genesis chapter four brings forth another powerful question, "Where is your brother Abel?" (Gen. 4:9). A similar alongsider coaching question might be, "Where are other people in this issue?" The context reveals that the question sets the stage for Cain to fess up and repent, an opportunity at which he failed. He had murdered his brother. We will unlikely find others in that scenario, but there may be bitterness, anger, or hatred that need to be brought into the light through similar questions. The alongsider coach might ask, "Where are you and where are other people?" Or, "Where is your Love for God and where is your love for people?"

There are few things as powerful as a well placed question. Powerful questions cultivate curiosity and get beyond just the seeking of information. Powerful questions seek out understanding. Powerful questions express immediate concerns about actual situations within the context of relationship, and demonstrate care and compassion for the individual being coached.

There are loaded questions and empty questions. There are good questions and there are bad ones. The Devil asks bad questions to draw us away from God. God asks good, powerful questions to draw us *to* Himself. The first question in the Bible

> *God asks good, powerful questions to draw us to Himself.*

was actually a very bad question, asked by Satan, "Did God really say…?" (Gen. 3:1). It is good to question everything from the kingdom of darkness, often revealed by bad questions. It is never a good idea to question what God says. In fact, we need to be rooted in God's Word, asking God for wisdom, listening first and foremost to Him, listening always with a third ear tuned in to the Holy Spirit.

Discern Telling Opportunities

Advice giving can limit people and get them stuck with what you know. Giving advice prematurely can derail the opportunity for a person to experience the power of God-initiated breakthroughs. It is usually easier to give advice and proclaim truth than to think of a good question to help a person discover what God knows. If we can ask a question to help a person hear from God, that is more effective. However, there are lots of examples of coaches in the Bible exercising significant telling. Although it should not be the automatic default to give advice, coaching does involve talking and discussing beyond questions.

I'm thankful for the times in my life when a good coach discerned my need for some coaching in a particular skill which involved some telling. When I took up shooting trap and skeet, I needed a coach. First, Randy showed me the details of operating the particular shotgun at hand. He gave me some tips, and then stepped back. As I pulled the trigger on clay pigeons, he coached me with good questions. "Where were your eyes when you fired?" "How do you feel about your follow-through?" How were you feeling when you said, 'Pull'?" What was on your mind after you pulled the trigger? His good coaching questions were preceded by some helpful skill instruction. He also told me some great stories about his own journey toward becoming a trophy winning trap and skeet competitor.

When wisdom reveals the need for telling, don't unload the whole truck at once. I heard somebody say once that there is a time to not say anything, and there is a time to say something, but there is not time to say everything. Telling a story can be powerful when the telling is concise and has a point.

> *When wisdom reveals the need for telling, don't unload the whole truck at once.*

Consider the story of Nathan with David. The prophet had a message to share with David. David needed to be confronted in his sin. The way the prophet went about that is insightful. Instead of bold accusation or probing questions, Nathan told David a story recorded in Second Samuel 12:

> The Lord sent Nathan to David. When he came to him, he said, "There were two men in a certain town, one rich and the other poor. The rich man had a very large number of sheep and cattle, but the poor man had nothing except one little ewe lamb he had bought. He raised it, and it grew up with him and his children. It shared his food, drank from his cup and even slept in his arms. It was like a daughter to him. Now a traveler came to the rich man, but the rich man refrained from taking one of his own sheep or cattle to prepare a meal for the traveler who had come to him. Instead, he took the ewe lamb that belonged to the poor man and prepared it for the one who had come to him." David burned with anger against the man and said to Nathan, "As surely as the Lord lives, the man who did this deserves to die! He must pay for that lamb four times

over, because he did such a thing and had no pity."
Then Nathan said to David, "You are the man!"[11]

The table was set by the prophet in the telling of a story. This became a powerful moment of repentance leading to restored faith. Nathan's example can inform our coaching. Rather than telling, why not try story telling? Even storying ourselves can be a powerful alongside coaching tool. Telling portions of our own story can build relationship and share a message without judgment. Letting God speak through our stories is powerful.

Jesus was very good at telling stories. He spoke in parables. He utilized visual aids like the fig tree or the coin in the fish's mouth. He talked about living

> *Jesus was very good at telling stories.*

water with the woman at the well. When Jesus taught and told stories, He was honest. He communicated truth. People need truth. They need to hear the truth, believe the truth, be taught the truth, and see the truth in action. Jesus declared Himself to *be* the truth (John 14:6). That is because all truth is embodied in His very person. He is the Living Word. The truth is alive, it is dynamic, and it comes to us through relationship with God and with each other. Truth telling fuels alongsider coaching.

Questions Open Doors

I was once coaching a Christ follower in a Thai restaurant. The fellowship and food were wonderful. I asked a simple question about his journey with Jesus, and he shared a powerful testimony of God's grace. During that interaction I noticed a man at a neighboring table listening intently to the conversation. He was obviously touched by the story of how God had worked in this young man's life. After our neighbor departed, the waitress came to our table and asked if we knew the man who had been sitting nearby. She informed us that the man had paid for our meal and wanted us to know that he was blessed by the story of how real God is and how His grace abounds. She enthusiastically handed us an envelope full of money that the man wanted to give us as a ministry donation. He had requested that we put the money in our church offering plate.

The waitress was so excited that she shared the story with most of the people in the restaurant that night. We didn't know the man, but God did. It was a divine appointment for my alongsiding friend, the gentleman near us, the waitress who was touched, and many others eating in the place that night. We never know the potential of an alongsiding coaching moment to have a contagious impact. It might start with a simple question complimented by active listening that ends up being a powerful and contagious encounter.

CHAPTER 6

CULTIVATING A COACHING CULTURE

A ship in harbor is safe, but that is not what ships are built for.
~William Shedd~

The best place for people to be coached and equipped for God's purposes is the local church. That doesn't mean just in a building, but within discipleship relationships. It is in the environment of faith communities where people are best discipled and equipped for embracing Jesus and engaging His mission. As Paul wrote in Ephesians:

> So Christ himself gave the apostles, the prophets, the evangelists, the pastors and teachers, to equip his people for works of service, so that the body of Christ may be built up until we all reach unity in the faith and in the knowledge of the Son of God and become mature, attaining to the whole measure of the fullness of Christ (Eph. 4:11-13).

Churches that focus on people as souls in need of discipleship are healthy places.

Churches which give people permission to serve are blessed. Promoting community and teamwork is the machinery which tills good soil for discipleship and worker growth.

Whether you are a pastor, lay leader, or new Christian, you can do something to help create an alongsider coaching culture. You might be God's instrument of the day. It can happen through prayer. Pray first, then step out and embrace alongsider coaching by investing in others who are willing to invest in others. When you see others doing it, celebrate and affirm them. Watch for people who might be interested and network them. Encourage older Christians to tell their story and live God's story in the presence of younger people and emerging workers who need to know the legacy of those who have gone before. "Even when I am old and gray, do not forsake me, my God, till I declare your power to the next generation, your mighty acts to all who are to come." (Ps. 71:18)

By the way, we have a current title for young workers, *emerging leaders*. We call the younger generation the *emerging generation*. The thrust behind those kind of descriptions is good, because we want to invest in those who are emerging on the fields of making a kingdom impact. However, just for clarification, those younger emerging leaders have more of a desire to *merge* their input into what older people have done and are doing.

I was flat on my back underneath an old suburban once, trying to fix the muffler. Things were not going very well, but I was working at it. A moment of frustration was interrupted by the sudden appearance of my younger son on his back next to me under the car. He looked over, saying, "Let me help, Dad." He was too young to contribute much, but his desire to work alongside his dad was so encouraging. The intentionality with which he merged his activity into mine was an inspiring relational moment.

One of the inspiring qualities I have noticed among younger leaders is a desire for healthy, authentic relationships. That is worth a merger discussion. There are brilliant, talented young people whose ideas need to be embraced and merged into what God is doing among older generations. Alongsider coaching is a critical piece for this to happen.

Coaching can take on various forms. We might find ourselves entering into a coaching relationship with a peer or someone younger. Sometimes coaching is upward, to those in authority. In Luke 2:49-50, Jesus used a powerful coaching question that issued forth respect and honor toward his earthly parents, Mary and Joseph. He asked them, "Why were you searching for me?" This is a powerful question for anyone, and it was asked with the necessary respect of "coaching up."

To successfully create an alongsider coaching culture will require careful consideration of obstacles. One of the potential roadblocks is time. Granted, we only have so much of it. But some things are worth saying "no" to in order to say "yes" to what is better, being about the Father's business. Growing disciples through alongsider coaching is certainly God's business. Besides, some of the activities that keep you busy can be done alongside other people you want to invest in.

Another obstacle is feeling inadequate. "I'm not qualified to coach others." "I'm not articulate enough to speak into the lives of other people." Moses tried that one (Exod. 3). Joshua must have felt inadequate, because God told him repeatedly in the first chapter of Joshua to "Be strong and courageous." When Jesus invited the disciples on the journey to become fishers of men, He said, "Don't be afraid" (Luke 5:10b). What God calls us to He also empowers us to do with courage. You can do this. Set your sails. You were built for it.

Organic and Not Linear

Coaching happens best as relationships develop, not as programs are applied. For coaching to be centered on the coachee, the coach must jettison all pre-agenda thinking that fails

> *Coaching happens best as relationships develop, not as programs are applied.*

to line up with the needs of the moment in the alongsider

relationship. As said well by Umidi, "The secret weapon of transformational coaching is that it is a transparent relationship—an organic, life-giving, empowering relationship."[12] This means a willingness to be flexible, adjusting coaching connections to meet the needs of the coachee in order to maximize key opportunities.

For coaching to happen, there needs to be the kind of relationships being formed which lend to agreement, permission, and commitment to unfold between people. Jesus trained his disciples not in a structured setting but by coaching in the classroom of life. He coached as they walked the journey together in relationship. This was organic and relational, not linear and institutional.

Sometimes the best alongsider coaching isn't planned. Often it takes place when we are praying for God to bring opportunities to invest in the lives of others. Other times a coaching relationship is intentionally established because a person has come to recognize the value of receiving coaching in the midst of a challenge they are facing or a skill they would like to develop. That means you should have strategically scheduled connection times, those are important, but don't miss opportunities in between those meetings.

In 2 Kings 3, there is a powerful story where the prophet instructs the kings to dig ditches so that when the water came it would have channels through which to flow (2 Kings 3:16). Even though they were in a desert, God brought promise. The provision came in His timing, and the land was filled with water (2 Kings 3:20). That is a great image to keep in mind for alongsider coaching. You may not see results right away as you walk with another person. There are dry seasons. Sometimes, you just help people to dig ditches so that when God's living water comes there are meandering channels for His grace to flow.

Crucible Coaching

In basic training for the United States Marine Corps, there is a valuable instructional experience called the "crucible." It is intentional training to help soldiers, and is a valuable training tool. It is designed to bring out the best through a combination of testing and team building. The training includes an intense week of situations that seem like they could kill you, but the activities are actually quite successful and productive because of the element of team and character testing.

It is strategic for coaches to step into those times when coachable people might be in a "crucible" experience. You may be able to identify a person ready for a coaching relationship as you observe a crucial time of need and teachability. There could be valuable opportunities to help them overcome fears, meet a challenge, learn the power of team, and even recast disaster into life lessons of real value. When a person is in the middle of a crucible experience, or coming out of one, there is strategic value in initiating a coaching relationship and stepping into an alongsider opportunity.

Thus, simply looking around for people on the training grounds of life will help identify those with whom coaches can come alongside. In simple terms, asking God to lead one into a coaching relationship and then watching for those opportunities as His appointments will go far in identifying the "who" of coaching.

Identifying a person to coach is often a simple response to his or her request. The most effective coaching relationships are initiated by the person wanting to be coached as he or she sees a need. If a person doesn't want to be coached, you can't coach them. However, potential coaches who are aware of people in need of coaching should feel free to take the

If a person doesn't want to be coached, you can't coach them.

initiative. That might come in the form of offering a prayer and making yourself available.

Another way to identify coachable people is to take notice of those who are investing in others. Paul communicated this idea to Timothy when he said, "And the things you have heard me say in the presence of many witnesses entrust to reliable men who will also be qualified to teach others" (2 Tim. 2:2-3). It is smart to entrust your time and energy to those able and willing to teach others. You would be wise to invest your time in people who are investing in other people.

> *You would be wise to invest your time in people who are investing in other people.*

Coming Alongside Emerging Leaders

As Jesus looked upon the crowds with compassion, He declared, "The harvest is plentiful, but the workers are few. Ask the Lord of the harvest, therefore, to send out workers into his harvest field" (Luke 10:2). This is an invitation to pray for harvest workers. God is answering prayers like that. He is calling forth workers. Those workers need alongsiding coaches. Pray for workers and coaches, and watch for them to show up. They are God's instruments for the building of His church and the expansion of His kingdom.

Coaches sitting with an emerging worker are in the presence of a potential answer to this kind of prayer. Jesus said these words to disciples who were direct answers to the divinely initiated appeal, and He sent them out. After instructing them, He went immediately to prayer: "I praise you, Father, Lord of heaven and earth, because you have hidden these things from the wise and learned, and revealed them to little children. Yes, Father, for this was your good pleasure" (Luke 10:21b). What a great lesson from Jesus the ultimate coach, to pray for emerging workers and to pray with emerging workers who may very well be answers to prayer.

There is a new generation of potential pastors, missionaries, and vocational workers waiting to hear the call, ready to say, "Here I am, send me" (Isa. 6:8b). Spiritual coaching has the potential to help them tune in to who God created them to be and how He wants them to serve. It could be argued that people in the world today are becoming dull of hearing and fail to help each other hear the call of God. We seem to carry around short clips on the video screen of the lives we live. Coaches in this regard can help people, in a relational context, to really listen for and hear God's dream for them. In the process, your calling might be clarified.

Answering the Call

When I was teaching elementary kids in a Christian school, one of my coaches encouraged me to take seriously the invitation of Jesus to pray for workers for the harvest fields. I tried to pray before class each day for the kids in my classroom, and often I would pray over the desk of each student, asking God to call forth His children into service, even as missionaries to the ends of the earth.

There came a day when I sensed the invitation, "Why not you?" So, my wife and I ended up being an answer to our own prayer for God to send forth missionaries. We began the application for overseas ministry. We spent about a year in prayer, planning and preparing for the possibility of going overseas as teachers in a missionary kid school. The morning of "the phone call" inviting us to consider moving to Dalat School in Penang, Malaysia, I was not fully prepared with an answer. We asked our leaders to give us time to pray about it, and went off to our teaching jobs for the day.

We asked significant friends and coaches in our lives to pray with us and for us. Deuteronomy 31:8 became a key verse that day in our wrestling, because I lacked courage. "The Lord himself goes before you and will be with you; he will never leave you nor forsake you. Do not be afraid; do not be discouraged." (Deut. 31:8) Friends encouraged us to "go for it." There was a growing sense of peace to say "yes." However, I asked God for one final sealing sign (some call it a fleece).

That evening I was talking with Kristi, and as we discussed our impressions of God's leading I began to randomly flip through our small town newspaper after having been encouraged to do so by a person who was like an alongside coach at that time in my life. To clarify the context, this newspaper was a small town publication which seldom contained much world news. This particular day, however, there was a significant picture of an open book with open hands that jumped out as an invitation. I noted the title, "In Good Hands," and read the words, "Two Malaysian Schoolchildren…." Kristi and I received that as a wonderful, powerful, providential circumstance that gave us courage to step into the calling to go to Malaysia as teachers. It was the exclamation point and punctuating circumstance we needed to put final confirmation to God's call. We departed several months later for a wonderful four-year term overseas as teachers for missionary children.

I would have missed an incredible blessing had I not opened the newspaper that day at the prompting of an alongsider coach. What if that person had told me what they had discovered rather than inviting me to discover it on my own? Alongsider coaching is about helping others to see God's fingerprints by prompting them to see what they might not otherwise take the time to see. The result can be powerful

Alongsider coaching is about helping others to see God's fingerprints.

shortcuts to transformational growth in the journey of becoming a disciple of Jesus.

If high school students had coaching in life purpose before graduating, they could be transformed. If college students had life purpose coaching in their first year, it could help them choose a more fitting career path. If soldiers had intentional coaching after a season of war, their adjustments could be smoother. If all missionaries and church planters were coached by people who had been there, their ministries could be enriched. If every emerging worker was coached through the ministry preparation process the way Jesus coached his disciples, the kingdom impact and the fruitful fulfillment in each worker would have phenomenal potential. As Joseph Umidi writes in *Transformational Coaching*, "The bride of Christ has the value base and heart motivation to become the most powerful source of highly relational and authentic transformational coaching to both its members and its surrounding community in the next decade and beyond."[13]

Communities of faith can and must do a better job of preparing people for ministry in a way that edifies and builds up local churches and expands the kingdom. This is an exciting challenge to be embraced with enthusiasm. The local church is the place to teach and model love for God and each other, sustaining the centrality and supremacy of Christ, flowing into mission. The local church is the place where people and gifts are expressed to equip them for ministry. The local church is the place where people discover the mission and are geared up to engage it, answering the call.

At the end of the book of Deuteronomy, Moses handed off the ministry to Joshua. As the Scripture says it, "Now Joshua son of Nun was filled with the spirit of wisdom because Moses had laid his hands on him. So the Israelites listened to him and did what the Lord had commanded Moses" (Deut. 34:9). We must hand off the baton to the next generation. Alongsider

Coaching is a great arena for expressing that we believe in them.

Coaching the Call of God in the Context of Community

Certainly there are higher callings, but every disciple of Jesus has a calling. The primary calling is to the person of Jesus. Flowing from that is the calling to follow Him into service, becoming all you can be in Christ, with works of ministry as the overflow (Eph. 4). Service is contagious to the building of the church and unto the fishing for people who need to be reached and discipled to discover God's call for them.

McManus calls it the "Jonathan Factor" in his book, *Seizing Your Divine Moment.* He uses Jonathan as the example to demonstrate the value and wonder found in latching on to God's perfect will for us in the opportunities that come our way. He points out that three words separate Jonathan from most of us, "Come, let's go."[14] This comes from a powerful story found in 1 Samuel chapter fourteen. Declaring a desire to take on the enemy, Jonathan invites his young armor-bearer onward and upward for an overwhelming challenge against all odds. Those words, "Come let's go," are the "Jonathan Factor" that moves people forward with confidence into the future.

"Come let's go."

Alongsider coaching can help people to discover God's will for the moment and His calling for the journey ahead.

There is a deep sense of joy when we tap into the call of God, a calling that unfolds according to the way He wired us. As Eric Liddell said in the movie, *Chariots of Fire*, "When I run, I feel His pleasure."[15] With this statement, he was tapping into an aspect of the call of God. Joy is a product of running with God, living in the center of His will, and tapping into the strength of His design.

Parker Palmer, in his book, *Let Your Life Speak*, suggests a combination of both the vocation and the calling of God. Vocation itself is not a goal that we pursue but a calling that we hear. First there must be the discovery of who we are, listening to God's voice in that regard. It is only after listening to our lives revealing who we are that we can give our lives the direction to go. Thus, the idea of vocation is not entirely separated from the idea of calling.

The idea of God's calling is actually the premise of Christian existence itself. In his book, *The Call*, Os Guinness contends, "Calling means that everyone, everywhere, and in everything fulfills his or her (secondary) callings in response to God's (primary) calling."[16] We are all to be doing "God's work," whether as pastors, missionaries, or factory workers. Like the model of the early Puritans, this gives everyday work a dignity and spiritual significance. A goal of alongsider coaching is to help people purposefully discover God's purpose for them, flowing out of the calling *to* Him.

Most of us have heard stories about people fleeing the calling of God. That might be because of personal desires that derail God's better desires, because of relationships that have taken priority over the relationship with God, or because of fear. I can relate to that one.

I was lost in the wilderness once. We were nearly thirty miles by horseback in the middle of the Bob Marshall Wilderness. I had packed in with a good friend who had been an outfitter in that area. We had tied up the horses and taken different paths on foot to look for elk. I hunted alone until early evening. It gets very dark in the wilderness after sunset. I didn't know where my partner was. I started walking the several mile journey back to the horses and got lost. I tried making my own way, unwilling to admit my dilemma, too proud to give in.

I managed to find the horses after several hours, and by horseback I tried following a path that I thought were the hoof prints from our journey into the area. I let the horses carry me on their own, thinking they could figure it out. Not so. Fear grew as I realized that we were even more lost. I knew by the odor of the sweating horses that they were wearing out.

Sitting on a stump hours later (stumped), on a very dark night because of the cloudy skies, I was cold and out of strength. People die in similar situations much closer to civilization, and I was in the middle of the wilderness. It was so quiet, except for the sound of the horses catching their breath and the trees making cracking sounds from the bitter cold.

As I sat on the log, stumped and crippled by fatigue and fear, a full moon suddenly broke through the clouds. There was light in the darkness. I could see enough of the terrain to continue on. God filled me with courage, and the only thing I remember about the rest of that night was walking step by step in total faith that God would get me back to camp. He did. I also remember entering the camp tent where I found my friend praying for me and waiting with expectancy.

That story is in many ways reflective of my life. I had done the same before coming to faith in Jesus, making my own selfish way through life, lost in the wilderness but unwilling to face it. I had also followed the paths of other people. I thought they knew where they were going, but they got me even more lost. My life was headed to an empty, dark place. I felt hopeless, empty, and afraid. The wilderness experience reminded me of the value of boldly facing fears in the light of God's strength. Walking forward and entering into the place of the fears that I wanted to avoid was the path to conquering them. Otherwise, those fears would have dominated my life. You can help others in that regard by coming alongside them and praying for them, waiting in prayerful anticipation of what God will do, as my friend did for me.

Stepping into the call of God is not without fear. Courage is fear prayed up. Prayerful coaching can help people to overcome fears in God's strength, for He is an audience of one, and we have, as Guinness states, "nothing to prove, nothing to gain, nothing to lose."[17] Stepping into the calling of God is a step into freedom! It is the culmination of a journey to embrace all that God has designed for us to be. We are set free for the calling to become more like Jesus, with ever-increasing glory, under the controlling work of the Holy Spirit. As the Scripture declares, "Now the Lord is the Spirit, and where the Spirit of the Lord is, there is freedom. And we, who with unveiled faces all reflect the Lord's glory, are being transformed into His likeness with ever-increasing glory, which comes from the Lord, who is the Spirit" (2 Cor. 3:17-4:1).

Establish Goals

When an alongsider coaching relationship begins or moves to a place which is more intentional, it is a good idea to establish some goals. Having a discussion up front about targets is important. These learning goals should be achievable, but you should not allow this to limit your faith for bigger goals. Bob Buford, in his book, *Game Plan*, mentions the significance of the "B-HAG," a "Big Hairy Audacious Goal."[18] A coaching relationship can usher in a contagious excitement for embracing a mission that is bigger and scarier than business as usual. This takes a combination of wisdom and faith. A good coach will help a coachee dream big and learn how to take steps of faith toward a future full of God's promises, while at the same time not allowing a big aim to cause the neglect of setting goals along the way that are measurable and achievable.

Effective leaders and coaches spend their most productive time by investing in coaching relationships with people who are growing by setting goals for themselves. Effective coaches are encouraged to serve as

Effective coaches are encouraged to serve as catalysts.

catalysts, helping coachees multiply their character and talents. As Marcus Buckingham and Curt Coffman express in their book, *First Break All the Rules*, "The time you spend with your best is, quite simply, your most productive time."[19] This must be done intentionally. It will not happen by accident. Setting goals is important.

Alongsider Elevating

Staying on the eleventh floor at a hotel during a recent conference, I headed out early for a breakfast meeting. After pressing the button for "lobby," I started to exit after the elevator stopped. I quickly noticed that I wasn't at the lobby. A lady getting on noticed my puzzled look and commented, "We're on the third floor. Yup. Happens to me all the time. Ya press the button and think you're gonna land where you intended."

It happens in life, too, doesn't it? We don't always end up where we expect. Have you ever stepped into a place which ended up being not what you anticipated? Sometimes that means a conversation with an unexpected person, sometimes it means a moment of anxiety, and always it takes a choice of faith with an awakened eye. Sometimes it means "pushing the button" on a promise of God you'd like to embrace for the day, with a surprise at the hallway God takes you down to get there. Sometimes there is a trial where character is developed, a green pasture where needed rest is welcomed, or a quiet stream of refreshing where a new step in the faith journey is embraced. By faith we step into whatever God may have for us when the door opens into a new adventure.

Churches need elevators. Communities of faith need alongsider coaches who will walk with others in such a way that their spirits are lifted and they gain access to God's elevated perspective, His wisdom. When we discover that, who knows what God will do. As an alongsider coach, you can serve as an elevator in God's empowering hands.

CHAPTER 7

MISSIONAL ALONGSIDER COACHING

Come, follow me, Jesus said, and I will make you
fishers of men.
~Mark 1:17~

Alongsider coaching may take the form of coming alongside a person who has yet to discover the beautiful life of following Jesus. Listening well, asking powerful questions, and praying for people are powerful coaching tools for an active witness. The scary "E" word, evangelism, is less threatening when seen in a relational alongsider context. Missional alongsiding means coming alongside people in a relational context to help them find abundant life. It is a significant way to accomplish what Jesus invites us to, fishing for people.

I'm a fisherman, and I know that some fish are hard to catch. I've also discovered that some kinds of fishing will require a more adventurous spirit. Younger relatives of ours were telling us stories about a sport they have become excited about, "hogging" for catfish (some call it "noodling"). I suppose it acquired that name because of the size of catfish they catch in muddy waters, "hogs." The fishermen find a hole where big catfish hang out. First, a big catfish is located. This is accomplished either by wading around with feet as the sensory locators or by swimming and probing with careful hands. Then, the daring fisherman can stick a hand down the throat of the fish and let it clamp on, bringing the big creature to the surface. Or, the brave "hogger" grabs the bottom lip and wrestles the big guy into the boat or onto the shore. There is danger of bites, being barbed, or the mistake of latching on to a critter that may not be what you thought.

Why would people fish like that? The excitement of an uncommon challenge? The thrill of all the unknowns? The adrenalin rush required to survive? Because risk-taking adventure is what people are built for? For the shared celebration of a good catch and the cheering of supporters on the other end of cameras in the boat or along the shoreline? Perhaps there are different strokes for different folks, but convincing proof could be presented for all of those reasons when the discussion shifts to fishing for people.

You can't take the analogy too far because people are infinitely more loved and beautiful than catfish, but fishing for people can lead to celebrated opportunities in helping our friends escape from the muddy holes they are trapped in. We all know people who think they are okay and comfortable, but they seem stuck in the mud of life. Other friends may be spending all their time and energy in the murky, empty endeavors of protecting nest eggs. There is something exiting and adventurous about helping people find freedom from the captivity of dark, muddy places. Fishing for people and becoming an alongsider coach means helping those around us to find fulfillment and purpose in the fresh and living waters of a relationship with Christ.

There is also cause for celebration when a person we are walking with comes to faith in Jesus and is rescued from deadly waters. In the parable of Luke 15, there is rejoicing and celebration in heaven and on earth when the lost was found. Only Jesus can take us into deeper places of hope and joy, and following Him includes the invitation to be a fisherman, fishing for people in need of the abundant life that He alone can bring. That kind of fishing leads to heavenly celebration, and it is well worth every effort no matter how muddy we get. Helping people find the delight of swimming in the ocean of God's grace is a high honor. My nephews tell me that hogging is fun. It is an adventure. Can fishing for people be fun? What do you do for fun? Who can you invite to join you? Missional alongsiding can feed excitement. We are wired for it.

Can fishing for people be fun?

Take Courage in Community

It does take courage to be an alongsider, sometimes no less courage than it takes to wrestle a large catfish to the surface. Sometimes people don't want to leave the mud of life. Yet, Jesus invites us to the world of fishing.

In Luke chapter five, Jesus was standing by a lake. The people were crowding around Him as He taught them. Jesus climbed into a boat, not because He was irritated by the crowds but because He was about to teach a powerful lesson. I used to think He got into the boat because people were crowding Him and He wanted to get a little breathing room. Actually, I believe He boarded the craft and sat down to teach in order to set the stage for illustrating a powerful multiplication truth.

I like the image of Jesus climbing into the boat. That scene is powerful. I came to understand on a turning-point day of my life that unless Jesus took over as the Captain of my life boat, I was on a sinking ship headed nowhere. At the invitation, He took control of my life and I now understand what it means to be rescued from the floodwaters of darkness and given purpose on an Ark of safety that is going somewhere. My life is no longer sinking. I can endure stormy seas with Him at the helm. I have direction and destination along with warnings of dangers on the radar. I could never go back.

We need the presence of Jesus, so we are promised the presence of Jesus. He is our greatest need and so our greatest promise. When Jesus commanded at the end of the book of Matthew, "Go and make disciples of all nations" (Matt. 28:19a), He also promised His presence as they embarked upon mission. "And surely I am with you always, to the very end of the age." (Matt. 28:20b) That is a wonderful promise. When we are fishing for people and coming alongside them with compassion without agenda, making ourselves available to disciple them, we can be assured of the presence of Jesus in that boat with us.

The fishermen in this story of Luke chapter five needed the presence of Jesus in their boat, as well as His instructions. He told them, "Put out into the deep water, and let down the nets for a catch" (Luke 5:4). They hesitated, because they had *"Put out into the deep water."* worked all night and hadn't caught a thing. But because Jesus told them to, they obeyed. They caught so many fish that they had to call for another boat, and the boats began to sink with so many fish. In the face of a miracle, they were astonished. Jesus encouraged them, "Don't be afraid; from now on you will catch men" (Luke 5:10). They became fishers of people walking in contagious witness, drawing people alongside and into the kingdom.

Those early fishermen needed fishing tackle, in their case working nets. Equally, you need to put to use what you have. You need to learn what those tools are, along with the self-awareness of your fishing style. Learning how to fish for people and share your faith can happen in many different ways. Whatever your style, you need to discover what it is and work at it. It's the invitation Jesus extends to us. It doesn't require advanced training or a theological degree. I learned to fish by watching others and then doing it. Fishing for people can be learned the same way.

I would love to be able to use nets, which require partners. That's what happened in this Luke story, they called their partners for help. James and John were referred to as Simon's "partners." Missional alongsiding happens best with other friends. Mission doesn't happen in isolation, it takes place in community. Consider what Lesslie Newbigin argued:

> I have come to feel that the primary reality of which we have to take account in seeking for a Christian impact on public life is the Christian congregation. How is it possible that the gospel should be credible, that people should come to believe that the power which has the last word in human affairs is represented by a man hanging on a cross? I am suggesting that the only answer, the only hermeneutic of the gospel, is a congregation of men and women who believe it and live by it. I am, of course, not denying the importance of the many activities by which we seek to challenge public life with the gospel—evangelistic campaigns, distribution of Bibles and Christian literature, conferences, and even books such as this one. But I am saying that these are all secondary, and that they have power to accomplish their purpose only as they are rooted in and lead back to a believing community.[20]

Somebody once said that it takes a village to raise a child. It takes a community of faith, a faith family, to make disciples. Walking in partnership with others who have missional passion in fishing for people is a fulfilling journey. Partnering with other people who desire to be missional coaches is powerful and effective. It is also a great adventure.

It also takes some level of courage to be a fisherman and an alongsider coach. There is a reason that Jesus said in Luke 5, "Don't be afraid." The truth is, we do get afraid. We do doubt ourselves. Fishing for people and with people can be scary. You might feel inadequate and carry fears that could hold you back. What if you find yourself reaching out to people who might bite? What if you get stuck in the mud or the black hole of a question you don't know the answer to? To be a missional alongsider coach means you need to hear the voice of this passage, "Don't be afraid."

Missional Listening and Asking Questions

I remember being at the recycle center where I struck up a conversation with another person who was depositing a big box of empty aluminum cans. I asked him what his motive was for recycling, why does he do it? The question presented an opportunity. I have always thought that taking care of creation and doing my part to recycle resources is an act of worship. Followers of Jesus have a higher motive for creation care and stewardship of what God has made. He created people, and engaging them in non-threatening conversations is a way to fish for men as an act of worship.

From active listening and asking powerful questions can emerge a potent witnessing platform to help launch a person into the place of grace. Listening and asking questions of interest are a gift that we can give to people who are processing life. Listening to a person's story with interest will provide the opportunity to share our story, one of the most powerful witnessing tools available to us. Our story about what God has done in our lives is a major part of our fishing tackle. What God is speaking to us through His Word and how He is shaping us is the key component of our witness. If we have a relationship with people, they will be interested in our story. Telling how our story has become a part of HIS story can be transformational.

Missional or evangelistic coaching also means slowing down, answering questions people might have. That doesn't mean you need to have all the answers. In fact, it is good to realize that some questions are simply smokescreens to avoid truth. A rich man came to Jesus one day and asked him, "Good teacher, what must I do to inherit eternal life?" The response of Jesus is a coaching response. He answered a question with a question. "Why do you call me good?" (Mark 10:17-18). Even though the man didn't respond well and went away sad, Jesus helped him discover what is really good. He was missing something better, connected with the goodness of God. Jesus slowed down, answered a question with a question to get to truth, and that lesson had an impact on many others.

Randy Newman shares in his article, "Stop Answering Questions," about a time when somebody to whom he was witnessing challenged him, "So, I suppose you think that people who don't agree with you, like all those sincere followers of other religions, are going to hell!" Rather than moving into a defensive mode or preaching with a quotation of Scripture, he responded with a wise, diffusing question, "Do you believe in hell?" Newman comments, "As long as we are on the defensive, the questioners are not really wrestling with issues. They're just watching us squirm."[21]

One of my favorite missional questions is to ask, "What has been the greatest challenge you have faced, and how did you get through it?" Sometimes, careful listening to the answers people give can offer snapshots of the fingerprints of God. Like the old chorus we used to sing, "He was there all the time." Psalm 139:13 says, "For you created my inmost being; you knit me together in my mother's womb." That is a fairly clear statement that God knows everything about us even before we are born. He knits people together, and carefully listening to a person's story can help you detect God's work. It is good to recognize that everyone is on a journey, and God is not willing that any should perish. He is working to draw people to Himself. Join Him.

The Idea of Journey

Early Christians were called people of "the Way" (Acts 9:2; 19:9, 23; 22:4; 24:22). That term pictures movement. Terms like driveway (you might wonder why we park there if it's a drive-*way*), pathway, walkway, freeway, right-of-way—all communicate movement. People who follow Jesus are on the right path walking with freedom in Christ. Being called people of the Way identified followers of Jesus as being on a journey.

The conversion of those first disciples could be said to have been about journey. In fact, one could identify two main types of conversion in the New Testament. First, there is the Pauline type of conversion, a dramatic encounter with Christ that can be identified with a point in time. It is characterized by a dramatic transformation in the context of a particular place and time.

A story with this type of conversion roots the experience in a particular event and time that is easy to talk about. The challenge, however, is that a person espousing this type of conversion may never get beyond it to the new and beautiful spiritual experiences at the hand of God in the life Jesus promised. This is especially true if it was an experience rooted in securing a heavenly future rather than embracing the abundant life in Christ in the here and now. Alongsiders can make all the difference in helping people to move forward in their conversion to deeper places in the journey with Jesus by the empowering of His Spirit.

The other type of conversion is a gradual experience that is marked by the idea of journey. Consider the twelve disciples, both in their conversions and in the coaching with which Jesus took them forward to become all they could be in Him. It is not clear exactly when they were saved. Was it when they responded to His invitation to follow? Was it later? Certainly it could be argued that their experience, unlike Paul's, was more of a journey.

Coaching can help people discover where they are in their relationship with Jesus in order to embrace Him and His mission with more enthusiasm and share His message with joy, being inspired as they focus on their unfolding story as a part of His story. Coaching is the process of walking alongside others at a certain season in their journey. The effective alongsider coach will give careful thought to where the coachee is on that journey and what "next steps" are being ordained by the Father.

There is much to be said about keeping in view the idea of journey as we are coached and as we coach others. Enoch and Noah didn't just hang around, they "walked with God" (Gen. 5:22-24; 6:9). When Jesus walked with two of the disciples on the road to Emmaus, it was the culmination of a journey He had already taken with them before the cross. The invitation of Jesus to follow is an invitation to travel down the road with Him and join in His work of making disciples.[22] This compelling bid is to make disciples, not just converts.

Journeys have some sense of direction. Without vision and purpose, people perish. They wander around with no meaning (Prov. 29:18). Jesus asked the disciples on the Emmaus road, "What are you talking about as you travel?" In other words, what is on your heart as you journey on the Jesus road? Alongsider coaching can help people discover where they are, who they are, and learn to listen to God's guiding voice.

A Not Easy Adventure

I went fishing on the first day of a camping trip in Wisconsin. The lake had shallow shores with weed beds, so it was very difficult to cast far enough to reach the deeper water where the fish were. No motorized boats were allowed, and we had no raft or canoe. So, I started wading out into the lake, more out of a desire to catch fish than a sense of adventure or demonstration of courage. The experience was not bad at first, but then the muddy bottom got really yucky. I sank knee deep in the muck, with the water about chest high. That was as far as I could go, and it was really hard to pull my feet out to take another step. I almost got stuck, and I couldn't stand in one spot too long without sinking into the mire, air bubbles rising to tickle my thighs. I kept imagining what might be hiding in the weeds and mud around my legs. Snapping turtles? Leaches? Snakes? Biting bugs yet to be discovered? Would I keep sinking and slowly disappear with no trace except my hat as a floating remnant?

From this nasty position, however, I caught a nice bass. I had to get into the muck and get uncomfortable to catch the bigger fish. That is much like fishing for men, I suppose. When Jesus said, "Come, follow me and I will make you fishers of men"—He didn't describe that as being an easy skim along the surface from the safety of a boat task. I guess sometimes we need to get out in the deeper water and wade through the crud to reach the fish that are hungry and ready to bite into the gospel and be coached life on life.

I hope that you are having opportunity to share your faith in the midst of whatever sludge is in your path. When Jesus indicated His desire to make us fishers of men, He didn't say it would be a pleasure cruise. It takes courage.

"Come, follow me,' Jesus said, "and I will make you fishers of men." At once they left their nets and followed him.
~Mark 1:17-18~

CHAPTER 8

ALONGSIDER DISCIPLEMAKING

We must do something about the cross, and one of two
things only we can do----flee it or die upon it.
~A.W. Tozer~

Matthew 28:16-20 contains wonderful words, meaningful marching orders from the head coach. He invites us to "make disciples." Actually, this is an imperative command. It solicits the question, "How do we make disciples?" He gave us the *what* and empowers us to figure out the *how*, within our context, in the power of His Holy Spirit.

We are to make disciples in a context that includes doing it *together*. There were eleven disciples hearing that command. "They" is repeated in the passage. An obvious plurality should be observed. It is about teamwork and relational discipling. It is my deep conviction that the most effective way to build disciples who are following Jesus in a genuine way is through relational alongsider coaching. People experience multiplied growth in their own lives when they embrace the joy of disciples helping other disciples of Jesus to be better disciples of Jesus.

This kind of disciplemaking through alongsider coaching is biblical. As it says in the book of Deuteronomy,

Hear, O Israel: The Lord our God, the Lord is one. Love the Lord your God with all your heart and with all your soul and with all your strength. These commandments that I give you today are to be upon your hearts. Impress them on your children. Talk about them when you sit at home and when you walk along the road, when you lie down and when you get up (Deut. 6:4-8).

This command emerged in an oral, verbal culture that was to be lived out in the context of families and friends as they walked in the daily routines of life. They were to be rooted in the Word of God, talking about the Scriptures at home and when they walked the way with others.

Those early practices still have valid, practical applications for us today. Making disciples happens best in the classroom of life. Talking about God and His word while walking alongside other people is powerful and transformative. It's what Jesus did with the disciples along the road to Emmaus. He opened the Scriptures to them (Luke 24:27, 32). This doesn't mean we have to be Bible experts, but it does mean sharing what God is teaching us through His word and how He is transforming our lives. As Tim Chester and Steve Timmis say it,

> We should be teaching one another the Bible as we are out walking, driving the car, or washing the dishes. People should learn the truth of justification not only in an exposition of Romans 5 but as they see us resting on Christ's finished work instead of anxiously trying to justify ourselves. They should understand the nature of Christian hope not only as they listen to a talk on Romans 8 but as they see us groaning in response to suffering as we wait for glory. They should understand the sovereignty of God not only from a sermon series on Isaiah but as they see us respond to trials with 'pure joy' (James 1:2). We have found in our context that most learning and training takes place not through programmed teaching or training courses but in unplanned conversations—talking about life, talking about ministry, talking about problems.[23]

Alongsider disciplemaking happens as we read the Word of God, study the Word, meditate on it, and let God transform us as we obey, sharing what He is doing with others. When two or three people are in an alongsider relationship where they read the Bible together, hunger for feeding on God's word can be contagious. Great discipleship takes place through informal out-of-the-classroom conversations rooted in Scripture. When people are asking and re-asking what God's Word is speaking into their lives and circumstances, transformation happens and growing disciples are formed.

Taking Up the Cross

While walking a mountain trail, my alongsiding friend shared a dream he had of the cross, its shadow, and Christians with their crosses in the shadow of the cross of Jesus. We talked about Jesus' command to take up our cross and follow.

> Then he called the crowd to Him along with his disciples and said, "If anyone would come after me, he must deny himself and take up his cross and follow me. For whoever wants to save his life will lose it, but whoever loses his life for me and for the gospel will save it." (Mark 8:34)

On the trail we spoke of the Father's view of us, the shadow cast from His radiance to us through the cross. We reflected on how He sees us through Jesus and His cross, if we will believe on Him. That day when I received Christ and His forgiveness and committed myself to His Lordship, I was forgiven and declared righteous. I was given life in the shadow of a redemption secured at Calvary. In that shadow of the cross, you are able to shift your eyes from self to Jesus, the author and perfecter of your faith. It is then the great privilege of a coach to walk alongside people who desire to journey in the shadow of the cross of Christ!

Denying yourself to follow Him is a minor task in the shadow of an exchange He made for you as the nails were pounded into His hands. We are to deny ourselves and take up our cross and follow Him. Talking about "self" in this way can seem heavy, but dying to self isn't so significant in the shadow of what Jesus did for us at the cross.

In the shadow of the cross we find the true Christ-life and its every blessing, flowing from His heart, from His outstretched arms in that expression of incredible love. As the song declares it, "….and the things of earth will grow strangely dim in the light of His glory and grace." As I look to the cross, I gaze upon His face and look into His eyes of compassion. In that moment, I see not just the shadow around me but the radiance beyond. The alongsider coach can help others embrace that light and explore what the cross life looks like on the journey of a disciple.

This self-denial doesn't mean I completely devalue myself. Dallas Willard brings forth a profound truth in his book, *Renovation of the Heart*: "Here is a very important point. Just because we are ruined doesn't mean that we are worthless. As a matter of fact, it is precisely our greatness as humans that makes our ruin such a huge shame. If we were insignificant, our ruin would not be so horrifying."[24] This comment captures an underlying theme emphasizing the value of our souls for making the process of renovation so much more significant and meaningful for God's glory. Jesus does not demean us or take away our dignity. Death to self, understood properly, is a key to restoration of the heart.

Death to self ushers in new life. In nature, the new emerges from death. Plants find nutrients in dying mulch. Seeds die to launch new plants. What happens in the natural gives a picture of the spiritual. Dying to self at the cross with Christ puts you on a road to new life. Walking that road with others is alongsider discipleship.

I reflected on Matthew 11:29-30 as I carried a heavy pack of elk meat out of the mountains, "Take my yoke upon you and learn from me, for I am gentle and humble in heart, and you will find rest for your souls. For my yoke is easy and my burden is light." I considered how heavy and yet insignificant is my "cross" in the shadow of the cross of Christ. After all, "A certain man from Cyrene, Simon, the father of Alexander and Rufus, was passing by on his way in from the country, and they forced him to carry the cross" (Mark 15:21). Which cross? The cross of Christ. What a great exchange. Your heavy burdens, those worries and cares that you sometimes carry alone like a backpack of heavy lifeless meat, cast to Him at the cross— in exchange for His life, carrying His life-giving gospel a bit further down the road.

At the cross we are yoked to Him. We identify with His suffering and death. You can do all things through Him who gives you strength as you release your grip on the baggage of self and take His yoke (Matt. 11:29-30). The world of self yokes a person to darkness and everything related to it. The yoke of Christ is one of love, peace, grace, mercy, and everything connected with true life and light. It is a crisis of exchanging me and mine for Him and His, a crisis of belief that yokes me with the Savior and places me in the power of his Lordship.

As Paul put it to the Corinthians (2 Cor. 4:8-11):

> We are hard pressed on every side, but not crushed; perplexed, but not in despair; persecuted, but not abandoned; struck down, but not destroyed. We always carry around in our body the death of Jesus, so that the life of Jesus may also be revealed in our body. For we who are alive are always being given over to death for Jesus' sake, so that his life may be revealed in our mortal body.

Does that sound like a light burden? Absolutely! I carry around the death of Jesus at the cross, His cross, that His life may be manifested in and through me as I live out His Lordship, yoked to Him alone in the shadow of the cross. It's the exchange that rolls the dark, dead stone off my back and releases me to be yoked in His resurrection life. These are the things of alongsider coaching that can help followers of Jesus to take up the cross for a great exchange. It is the path of discipleship. It is the way to experience intimacy with Him, to really know Him (Phil. 3:10-11). It is the goal of alongsider coaching, joining God in His work of transforming people to look more and more like Jesus—disciples.

Coaching Purity

One of the learning needs that cannot be taught or caught well in a formalized classroom is that of the righteousness that Jesus desires of His followers. Jesus said we are to seek first His kingdom and His righteousness (Matt. 6:33). That can happen in alongsider relationships where one person sharpens another as iron sharpens iron (Prov. 27:17).

I was prayer jogging along a river trail one night, leaning into a strong wind that was blowing dead leaves from the trees all around me. Every autumn the leaves drop and die, giving room for future growth and providing nutrients. Sometimes the wind speeds up the process. It is the cycle of things by God's design, flowing from His wisdom.

The thoughts of my heart kept rhythm with my pace as I considered how death cultivates growth. Denying myself fertilizes a maturing faith. Self-denial is a path which cultivates purity, making room for the righteousness of Christ in me as I shed those things that need to die. Sometimes the winds of our world provide a shortcut.

Randy Alcorn wrote a great book called, *The Purity Principle*. He put the purity principle in simple terms when he wrote, "Purity is always smart; impurity is always stupid."[25] Choosing the path of purity is always resourced in God's wisdom. Unrighteous choices are always foolish, self-destructive, and sometimes deadly. Purity takes us to a safe place. Impurity takes a person to very risky places. Purity always helps people. Impurity always hurts people, along with others around them.

When the winds of temptation gust in our direction, resisting is always wise. When struggles seek to blow us off track and when sin swirls around us, the wise choice is to stay rooted in Christ and His word. The smart decision is to dig deeper for grounding in His righteousness, lifting your eyes toward God as the source of help, elevated limbs in praise for His grace and strength. Standing firm brings a cleansing result, with the winds blowing off the dead stuff. That can mean a frozen winter season, but death to self is the path of purity and renewed abundant life. Standing in Christ and allowing the breeze to blow away the unnecessary sources of self-satisfaction can be a shortcut to the victorious life of purity.

Trees growing in clusters survive windy places. Magnificent forests are marked by groups of trees where roots are able to intertwine for added support. Alongsider coaches are necessary for the life God invites us into. "Since we have these promises, dear friends, let us purify ourselves from everything that contaminates body and spirit, perfecting holiness out of reverence for God." (2 Cor. 7:1)

Alongsiding and Teaching

In my experience growing up, learning about being a Christian happened mostly in church and Sunday school. Traditional models of discipleship have often been sanctuary or classroom oriented. Modern education, even in the church, too often assigns responsibility for learning upon the curriculum and the teacher. This puts the teacher in the place of authority and the learner in a submissive role. Although significant changes are being made in many places, this approach has been the main model for the American educational system. Adult learning has modeled that of childhood education.

Not that this is all bad. There is certainly a valuable place for the classroom approach. However, group instruction works best when complemented by smaller, more relational interactions that can be cultivated through alongsider coaching.

There is certainly a key role that group Bible studies, classroom discipleship, and preaching have in the process of making disciples. Teaching and preaching certainly play a key role. Teaching by lecture can be effective, but in some ways it can be like pushing on a rope. The flexibility offered through alongsiding can provide necessary wiggle room through channels which provide advances.

The proclamation of the Word is crucial to the development of a Christ-follower. Small group studies, cells, or life care groups (whatever you may want to call them) are very strategic and powerful for people to experience the growth which can happen in that context. Sunday school can certainly have a meaningful purpose in many cultures. In combination together and with alongsider coaching, what is learned in an instructional setting can be unpacked and applied through a small group or a coaching relationship with the intent to respond with specific prayer and the forming of action steps appropriate to a person's individual context.

The traditional classroom approach creates an environment where students are dependent on their teacher, increasing the gap between the need to be self-directing and the ability or motivation to be self-disciplined in the learning process. God created us with a will, and people are responsible for their own lives and learning needs. Alongsider coaches need to make the transition in their own minds to help those they are coaching move from dependency to self-direction and self-discipline in the discipling process. Helping people become self-feeders, in active pursuit of the God who is pursuing them, is a goal of alongsider coaching.

Andragogy

Andra-what? They actually have a name for the style of learning characteristic of the alongsider coaching model. "Andragogy" is the art and science of helping adults learn, operating under the assumption that adults learn best in informal, comfortable, flexible, *Adults learn best in informal,* and nonthreatening settings. *comfortable, flexible, and* Alongsider coaching, in this *nonthreatening settings.* regard, works best with approaches which emphasize the learning needs of the coachee. Coaching will have the goal of real learning in view, beyond education driven by curriculum.

People need to know why they need to know. There is a necessary desire to learn something before undertaking it with enthusiasm. In this regard, the alongsider coach would be wise to help the coachee arrive at the place of recognizing the need to know. When a coachee has a sense of need, the agenda of coaching and the learning process is put in his or her court.

People also have a greater readiness to learn because of the demands of real life which require new coping strategies for greater effectiveness in the workplace, at home, and for life in general. A strategy for effective coaching must consider the creation of learning opportunities in the context of real life experiences. It is not necessary for a coach to take on a passive posture, simply waiting for readiness to develop.

Intentional coaching can be strategic in creating an environment for growth. It is strategic to seize teachable, coaching moments to insure that the agenda is determined by coachee needs rather than being "teacher"-driven. People will learn best and grow best through the coaching relationship if there is motivation and readiness to learn. Umidi summarizes this well:

> The job of the coach, then, is not to choose a change agenda, but to allow the client to choose it based on what God is doing in his or her life. God must initiate the change by creating an experiential context that opens the individual up to change at a deeper level than usual. The coach simply helps the client identify these teachable moments instead of coming with an agenda.[26]

People are more likely to be motivated to learn and grow when they perceive benefit toward accomplishing real life goals and tasks with issues and problems. This understanding is already being applied with success in teaching youth in some schools. In Baltimore, Maryland, schools are emerging which are alternatives to traditional education. These charter schools are more like trade schools to keep kids enrolled in the educational process. When students are exposed to real-life careers and see the potential for a better life, they are motivated to learn how to read and do math because there are practical applications in their sights. In a similar way, offering a coaching relationship that is life-centered and skills-oriented can help coaches overcome obstacles to learning. If people don't perceive that coaching is connecting with their needs and interests, linking with what they care about, alongsider coaching will be empty.

This highlights a final issue in the world of andragogy, that of motivation. People are responsive to external motivators which include better jobs, promotions, higher salaries, and a better life. However, they are even more responsive to internal pressures, such as the

The posture of an alongsider coach is to facilitate Spirit-initiated discovery.

desire for increased job satisfaction, self-esteem, and a higher quality of life. The issue of motivation is a significant component for an effective alongsider coaching strategy. The posture of an alongsider coach is to facilitate Spirit-initiated discovery and Spirit-empowered motivation which moves a person forward.

Coaching Talents and Strengths

During my years on our high school football team, I remember making a huge mistake on the field under the Friday night lights. I anticipated the video being shown to the whole team the following Monday. I was nervous about the embarrassment that would come when the coach pointed out my blunder in front of the whole team. However, that moment of humiliation never came. The coach talked only about the good plays we accomplished as a team. I wonder if he had perhaps read some remarks of Vince Lombardi during that season, who said, "Individuals are always stronger when they have their successes and strengths clearly in mind."[27] Lombardi apparently had begun to show only the strengths and successes in film replays. A good alongsider coaching relationship involves a commitment to focus on strengths and celebrate the victories to God's eternal glory.

The book of Job is about a man who was tested and emerged triumphant. God articulated the strength of the Behemoth (Job 40:15) and the Leviathan (Job 41:1) in His discussion with Job. These animals glorify God in their strength, pointing to His greatness. It is not a stretch to say that disciples of Jesus also need to focus on the strengths that God has built in them, even when times are hard. When people discover those God-made strengths and focus on them in life and ministry, it is to the glory of His strong name. Psalm 139 offers some theology helpful for effective alongsider coaching:

For you created my inmost being; you knit me together in my mother's womb. I praise you because I am fearfully and wonderfully made; your works are wonderful, I know that full well. My frame was not hidden from you when I was made in the secret place. When I was woven together in the depths of the earth, your eyes saw my unformed body. All the days ordained for me were written in your book before one of them came to be (Ps. 139:13-16).

God weaves people together, within the mother's womb, a work that is wonderful, and coaching can help people to "know that full well." God builds strengths into a human being even before birth and He ordains each and all days. Strengths are things that you do well, and include patterns of behavior, thoughts, and feelings that bring satisfaction, pride, reward, and progress toward excellence.[28] When people operate in areas of strength, there is a genuine sense of joy as they live out what God has built into them, and coaching can help people operate in line with how He has knit them together.

Furthermore, redemption gives us a transformed identity, a sanctified new life which defines us as who we are "in Christ" (Rom. 12:5, 15:17; 1 Cor. 1:4, 30; Gal. 3:28; Eph. 1:3, 2:6; Phil. 3:3; Col. 1:28, 2:10). Good alongsider coaching helps people to discover God's hard wiring in them and the riches and strengths of God's glory in them through Christ. When coaching helps people discover not just who they are but "whose" they are, that is powerful. He is our hope, and He is a glorious hope.

The "strengths theory," the idea of focusing on strengths and managing weaknesses, is a major theme brought out by Donald Clifton and Paula Nelson in their book, *Soar with Your Strengths*. If people (or coaches and their coachees) develop their strengths to the maximum, the strength becomes so great that it will overwhelm the weakness.[29] Scientists could certainly discover and articulate the weaknesses in the Behemoth and the Leviathan, but the strengths overpower the weaknesses. Effective coaching can emphasize the same for people being coached.

Too often, people are driven by the desire to reduce or even hide weaknesses rather than focus on strengths. As Reggie McNeal said in a lecture at Fuller Theological Seminary, we are "pathology fixated." In other words, learning processes too often take us to a place where we are simply "better informed about our sickness."[30] Our society builds counseling services and talk shows around getting to the weak areas of our lives for fixing and adjusting. It is counterintuitive to focus on strengths, but critical to do so in order to lead people in discovering God's best for them in accordance with how He created them.

A caution is warranted as we consider the coaching of strengths in disciple-making. A strength can become a weakness if deployed incorrectly. Your greatest strength can become your greatest weakness. There are times that it will be appropriate to not operate in an area of strength when serving others, as they may be intimidated or robbed of the

> *Your greatest strength can become your greatest weakness.*

blessing of operating in their particular gifting. This means that loving servanthood and godly character must be appropriately encouraged as undergirding the application of strengths.

In the parable of the talents in Matthew 25:14-30, the management of assets is an important teaching, exhorting believers to be faithful in relation to their resources. This is not just about money or material things. The gifts, opportunities, talents, and strengths God gives you are among the key assets you are to manage, and effective coaching will draw them out. That means asking questions. What are the assets God has given you to manage for His kingdom glory? What people are in your life who might be divine appointments? Who could benefit from your leadership? What people in your faith community are assets to kingdom building?

In the parable of the gold coins in Luke 19:1-27, the primary lesson has to do with taking advantage of opportunities to serve the kingdom with zeal. Richard Clinton and Paul Leavenworth, in their book, *Starting Well*, write of a tension that must be held together: "On the one hand, we can take comfort that we will only be held accountable for what God has given us. He doesn't expect more out of us than we are capable of. On the other hand, the other parable [of the gold coins] stresses the fact that we are to push, learn, and grow so that we can take advantage of every opportunity. We are not to be complacent."[31] What opportunities are before you where you could apply your God-given strengths? That is a good alongsider question.

The talents that God has built into you are the most important raw materials for strength building. When you identify your most powerful talents and hone them with skills and knowledge, you are on the way to a "strong life."[32] How do you discover your strengths? Marcus Buckingham and Donald Clifton, in their book, *Now, Discover Your Strengths*, point out that how a person thinks about an activity can help identify a talent. "If all you are thinking about is the present—'When will this be over?'—more than likely you are not using a talent. But if you find yourself thinking in the future, if you find yourself actually anticipating the activity—'When can I do this again?'—it is a pretty good sign that you are enjoying it and that one of your talents is in play."[33]

The idea of discovering your strengths and focusing on them is so basic and yet so missed in our world. It makes so much sense to operate in accordance with the way God made you. Coaching can help others to discover the strengths that God has put into them and reinforce them with practice and coaching toward more productive, more fulfilled, and more successful service unto the King and for His glory.

Growing numbers of people today, in every culture around the world, are recognizing that they have a unique God-given dream and a unique design that they need to discover and express. There are key fingerprints of God that need to be drawn out and made known for other people to see.[34] People can be liberated by discovering God's imbedded grain in their lives. Many of these people are looking for the personal, one-on-one relational approach that coaching can offer. Coaching can help people to become more focused, adaptable, and resilient. When life changes and needs come on the horizon, they are less likely to be caught unprepared.

Managing Weaknesses

Along with focusing on strengths, we must recognize the need to manage our weaknesses. This is not easy, but necessary. Ignoring a weakness is a recipe for certain disaster, either for you or others or both. Clifton and Nelson discuss our fixation on weaknesses and how difficult it is to avoid fixing them: "Nevertheless, it's our culture's instinct to fix them, and so the idea of managing one's weaknesses, versus fixing them, is the most challenging part of the 'Strengths Theory.'"[35] This means that we do not expect weak areas to disappear, nor is our desire to "master" them. We must learn, however, to manage those weaknesses. A helpful attitude includes tapping into a solid sense of humor. Don't take your weaknesses too seriously. Don't take yourself too seriously. Remember, becoming a disciple is about denying yourself .

Here is a thought: Help others to discover what they do not do well, and help them stop doing it. What do you not do well? Look for ways to stop doing those things. Cease to engage in those activities that aren't strengths. A sailor would call that throwing cargo overboard. A sports coach might call it repositioning. A boss might call it a revision of the job description. It would be good coaching to help people stop putting themselves in situations where they consistently fail. Coaching can help in this process of discovery, learning how to manage weaknesses and focus on strengths. This might include helping a coachee to list the unenjoyable activities they are involved in and those that have not made a difference in their lives or the lives of others for a kingdom impact, and toss those things aside.

So, what about verses in the Bible that talk about God working through our weaknesses? Consider Paul's words, "If I must boast, I will boast of the things that show my weakness" (2 Cor. 11:30). Or in his epistle to the Romans, "In the same way, the Spirit helps us in our weakness. We do not know what we ought to pray for, but the Spirit himself intercedes for us through wordless groans" (Rom. 8:26). What about the verse, "But God chose the foolish things of the world to shame the wise; God chose the weak things of the world to shame the strong" (1 Cor. 1:27). These Scriptures indicate the other edge of a double-edged sword. There is a paradox. God builds strengths in us that He can draw out, and in our weakness He brings out strength to His glory.

It should also be noted that the context of many of these verses is that of suffering and life circumstances, not abilities or inabilities in the realm of gifts and strengths. When circumstances cause our weaknesses to be manifested, we can, through prayer and dependence on the Spirit, come out victorious and to God's glory. He shines as the light in the darkness, even with greater radiance when the circumstances are beyond our abilities. When life happens and weakness is manifested, God is our strength.

Character

The issue of character is vitally important to alongsider disciplemaking. Character is the gold nugget for discipleship. Talents and strengths without

> *Character is the gold nugget for discipleship.*

strong character is a Leviathan without restraint or a Behemoth's tail running wild. God-given strengths must be under God's reign. Strengths under the control of the Spirit will produce ministry fruit and effective leadership.

Coaching can help people to develop character as they study the Bible and submit to God's transforming work (Rom. 12:1-2). It means becoming like the Berean Christians, "Now the Bereans were of more noble character than the Thessalonians, for they received the message with great eagerness and examined the Scriptures every day to see if what Paul said was true" (Acts 17:11-12). Coaching in the arena of staying biblical can cultivate noble character.

Sometimes that means coaching people through times of trials and suffering, helping them in character development. This is identified in Paul's epistle to the Romans, "Not only so, but we also rejoice in our sufferings, because we know that suffering produces perseverance; perseverance, character; and character, hope. And hope does not disappoint us, because God has poured out his love into our hearts by the Holy Spirit, whom he has given us" (Rom. 5:3-5).

Clarifying the Calling

The important discipleship concept of "dying to self" (Luke 9:23-24) does not mean total conformity or putting aside the individuality God created me with (Ps. 139), but rather celebrating diversity in unity as I do my part in the greater body of Christ. That part in the church is a calling, and it needs to be clarified and coached.

As I have studied the calling of God over the years, I have discovered some key questions to help discern God's will for a particular decision or a particular calling. The first question to ask is whether a decision, option, or direction is rooted in Scripture. It is of fundamental importance to test everything with the word of God, and alongsider coaches can help with this. The primary way that God speaks to us is through the Bible.

A second question has to do with the righteous choice. As I seek first His kingdom and righteousness (Matt. 6:33), is this calling or decision arising in the secret closet of prayer? What choices will help me to be more like Jesus? God would never desire a purpose for us that contradicts His character or His desire for us to be more like Jesus. Sometimes a particular calling, in fact, has more to do with the shaping of a leader's character toward righteousness than about successful outcomes or immediate kingdom impact. It is wise for an alongsider coach to be aware that God sometimes calls people to a particular season of ministry to shape them for something else later.

A third question I like to ask is, "Is it right?" In other words, does this calling or decision fit with common sense? Does it match personal wiring? Do I have the necessary competencies? Do I have the character, competencies, and right cultural fit to go this direction? Is the chemistry right? Acknowledging that God knew us in our mother's womb, we also should realize that God builds into us that which we can do for His glory. This includes the question of personal requests and desires. Is it something I want, lining up with interest, passions, and personal desire?

Another question has to do with the confirmation of other people. It is important to receive the affirmation of people who know us well, confirming that we are headed in the right direction. Any calling should be affirmed and confirmed by godly, spiritual counsel.

A final question, last for a good reason, is to discern what God might be saying through circumstances. Sometimes God puts an exclamation point on a particular direction by orchestrating events and situations to confirm a decision or calling. It is good for an alongsider coach to probe what God might be saying through particular situations in which people find themselves.

To summarize, consider these questions in your coaching relationships to help people discover the particular path in a decision before them:

1. What is **Rooted in Scripture?** (Acts 1:15-22; Matt. 4:4, 19, 5:13, 6:33; Acts 1:20-22; Prov. 6:20-23, 8:10-11, 32-33, 9:10; Heb. 4:12)

2. What is **Righteous?** (Eph. 6:18; Acts 1:21- 26; Rom. 8:28-29; Matt. 5-6)

3. What is **Right?** (Acts 1:23-24; Prov. 1:1-3, 3:5-6, 4:11, 10:24, 21:1; Rom. 8:28; Ps. 139) {Character, competency, calling, culture, chemistry}

4. What best lines up with personal **Requests and Desires?** (Ps. 37:4; Prov. 19:21, 21:21)

5. What is being **Rightly Confirmed and Affirmed by Others?** (Acts 1:21-26; Ps. 1; Prov. 10:23, 15:22, 19:20; Heb. 13:7-8)

6. What is being **Revealed** and highlighted by circumstances? (Acts 1:15-26; Prov. 16:9, 33, 20:24)

CHAPTER 9

WHAT DOES A COACHED PERSON LOOK LIKE?

Where there is no revelation, the people cast off restraint; but blessed is he who keeps the law.
~Proverbs 29:18~

It has been said that if you don't know where you are going, you'll end up somewhere else. As the Bible puts it, without vision people wander aimlessly and perish (Prov. 29:18). In a factory, it would be silly to run production lines without workers having a clear vision of what the final product will look like. If you are effective at coaching another person, what might they look like at the other end of an alongsider relationship? What does a fully dedicated follower of Christ look like? What is a picture of success in terms of making disciples?

If being a disciple of Jesus consists of denying yourself, taking up the cross to follow him, the cross is a powerful image to build upon in developing a picture of a discipled, coached person. Consider the diagram on the next page, which offers an image of what a disciple's cross might look like. It is inspired by the discipleship Bible study by Avery Willis Jr. and Kay Moore, *The Disciple's Cross.* [36] Take up the cross as a picture of what a fully coached disciple is marked by.

Christ-centered character is at the heart of it all. Obedience and spiritual disciplines help keep us there. Prayer and worship is the upward orientation of the vertical beam of the disciple's cross. Prayer, worship, and grounding in the Scriptures are essential for cultivating a relationship with God. The horizontal beam is about relationships as we serve others in the church community and as we serve those in our neighborhoods and regions through missional engagement.

Each realm flows from the centrality of Jesus Christ. He is at the heart of life, and love for Him flows into love for His Word, love for God through prayer and worship, and love for people as we live on mission and serve others in the community of faith.

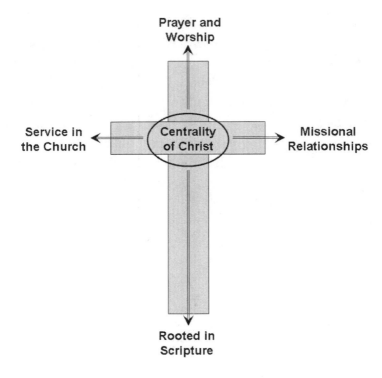

Christ-Centered Character

The Bible reveals Jesus as central for all truth and all true loving, inviting authenticity in the journey of following God into life. The people we coach must be marked by a passionate and contagious embrace of Christ in all His fullness. Coaching itself needs to be incarnational, living out the Christ-centered life.

Can passion for Jesus and Christ-like character be coached? I believe character can be called out, cultivated, and coached as we walk with others and make disciples. It flows from a life centered on Jesus, embracing a journey toward Christ-like character. Some refer to this as the golden nugget, the diamond, a key to ministry success in following Jesus. This doesn't mean perfection, but it does mean a hunger and thirst for God and His righteousness. That hunger reveals a heart in process, being shaped by the Creator.

Christ-centered character is essential in a disciple of Jesus. Maxwell pointedly writes, "The first thing to look for in any kind of leader or potential leader is strength of character. I have found nothing more important than this quality. Serious character flaws cannot be ignored. They will eventually make a leader ineffective—every time."[37] Essential character qualities needing to be identified, nurtured, and encouraged in a coaching relationship would include honesty, integrity, self-discipline, teachability, dependability, perseverance, conscientiousness, and a strong work ethic.

Sometimes issues of character derail disciples from arriving at the destination of their callings. As Umidi explains, "The reason why many who are gifted are not called to greater things is because talent and gifting will get you into areas where your character can't keep you."[38] Christ must be central, and everything flows from that.

How do you coach Christ-centered character? I am convinced that God builds character into people as life happens. This often means trials, seasons of pain, and challenges that stretch us beyond our means. There are many inspiring examples of people who overcame fears, met a challenge, and turned disaster into something of value as their character was developed through the process. Coaching people through strategic seasons of character development is powerful. It might mean just being there, it will include powerful questions and active listening, and must be bathed in prayer.

John chapter fifteen is a great passage to study with someone you are discipling. It revolves around abiding in Jesus, remaining in Him. As Jesus said it, "Apart from me you can do nothing" (John 15:5). As you seek to coach character, remember that balance comes by the empowerment of the Holy Spirit as we walk in the words of our Lord: "Love the Lord your God with all your heart and with all your soul and with all your mind" (Matt. 22:37-38).

Demonstrating a Love for the Scriptures

The vertical beam of a follower's cross must be rooted and established in God's Word. Life must be grounded in the truth of the Bible. Alongsider coaches must continually maintain this foundation. Jesus is the Truth, and keeping Him central means being a student of His Word.

When Jesus walked with those two disciples on that road to Emmaus, He opened the truth of the Scriptures as they journeyed along the way. "And beginning with Moses and all the Prophets, he explained to them what was said in all the Scriptures concerning himself" (Luke 24:27). What an intriguing scene, Jesus walking alongside two disciples revealing Himself to them and unfolding the revelation of the Old Testament. In Luke 24:32 they said to each other, "Did not our hearts burn within us while he talked to us on the road, while he opened to us the Scriptures?"

> "Did not our hearts burn within us while he talked to us on the road, while he opened to us the Scriptures?"

It is of primary necessity in our world today to coach a new generation of people who are grounded in the Scriptures and able to bring the whole gospel into their world with relevancy yet without compromise of truth. We must take deliberate action in conversations to move disciples of Jesus toward a greater love for the Word of God. We might be able to pass on some experiences to the next generation, we can tell our stories, but that which is lasting, steady, and completely relevant will be the written Word. Disciples must be competent in the Scriptures.

Related to solid understanding of the Bible, there must be an ability to live with paradox. An uninformed reader of the Bible might claim that there seem to be contradictions. In truth, there are no contradictions in Scripture, only apparent contradictions where two blades of truth are both equally true. It is a double edged sword which makes a piercing point (Heb. 4:12) —that is the idea of paradox. It is easier to sharpen one side or the other, but both blades of truth must be held together in tension. As one of my former seminary professors put it, "It is easier to move to a consistent extreme than to stay in the center of biblical tension."[39] Christ followers must be able to live with ambiguity, be flexible with the application of Scripture, be doers of the Word (James 1:22), and celebrate paradox without contradiction in the truth of the Bible.

As disciples grow in a love for the Scriptures, they must also be marked by tenacious obedience. Establishing coaching relationships that are real and relevant will help in this regard. Through biblical coaching, growing disciples can test and approve the perfect will of God.

Cultivating Love for God through Prayer and Worship

Consider once again the picture of a disciple through the image of the cross. To maintain the centrality of Christ there must be a love for the Scriptures which keeps people grounded and also draws the heart upward in love for God expressed in prayer and worship

It is by the discipline of prayer and worship that people remain focused and centered. Prayer and worship are called disciplines because that's what it often takes. It is a sacrifice of praise (Heb. 13:15). It costs something (1 Chron. 21:24). It is not always driven by good circumstances, great music, or positive feelings (Hab. 3:17-19). But the discipline of prayer and worship, no matter what, cultivates deeper love for God than circumstances of life can ever produce.

One of the initial ways to create a practice of prayer and worship is to feed the material of a person's experiences of the past into altars of celebration, helping in the process of recognizing God's sovereign hand beyond time. Coaching people by helping them to recreate their own stories is a way to feed into a life of recognizing God's work and praising Him for it. It is healthy and profitable to explore the drama that God has been weaving since before the beginning of time, which He has also placed in our hearts. Coaching can help others see that it's not just about Jesus becoming part of their story, but about their part in God's story. Becoming a part of God's bigger story brings a meaningful life of purpose. It takes you beyond yourself. It is a wonderful thing to fuel times of prayer and worship by remembering God's work in your past and be drawn into His magnificent drama.

Before any of our individual stories began, there was something wonderful already going on with God in control of a greater plot. Coaches recognize that life is about getting caught up in His story, which explains ours. That story is vitally connected with the stories expressed in the lives around us, particularly those we coach.

Cultivating love for God doesn't happen by accident. It is so easy in our world to eat spiritual junk food all day long. If the entertainment we feed on lacks substance and significance we get filled up with unhealthy rubbish. Then we get so filled up that there is no room left for God hunger. If we desire an appetite for God, we need to pray for it. We also need to coach it. Get rid of the junk food. Make room for God hunger. Cultivate love for God. Make a habit of fasting from anything that hinders healthy hunger. Fast from bite-sized joys and experience deeper life.

Healthy Living and Spiritual Disciplines

Christ-centered character which roots us in Scripture and fuels prayer and worship is cultivated through healthy living. That means spiritual health, emotional health, relational health, and physical health. Healthy living facilitates spiritual growth, emotional maturity, relational development, and includes taking care of our bodies. Emotional wellbeing means learning how to forgive and embracing the emotions God created within us, living with freedom and joy flowing from a sanctified imagination. Relational health means doing relationships God's way, with authenticity and in community. Physical health means treating our bodies as temples of the Holy Spirit and honoring God with our bodies (1 Cor. 6:19-20). Spiritual health means a holistic approach in caring for all components of the life God has entrusted to us. Healthy living means obedience to God's Word and practicing the spiritual disciplines.

> *Relational health means doing relationships God's way, with authenticity and in community.*

There seems to be a growing surge of interest in the spiritual disciplines of the faith. Prayer and fasting, Scripture meditation, worship, stewardship and giving, solitude, service, and other spiritual disciplines are attractive because they are avenues of what is real and keeps us rooted. Finishing well can be facilitated by faith practices which help to cultivate the deeper life. Wise spiritual coaches will put the spiritual disciplines up front as Spirit-driven means for authentic transformation of the heart, the mind, the body, the social life, and the soul. Too often these disciplines are only applied to the social life arena, like during worship services. The outward appearances should be an overflow of inner disciplines that flow from the heart.

Personal prayer retreats serve in the realm of cultivating spiritual disciplines. Stepping away from the demands of ministry and life to reflect deeply and prayerfully is a powerful practice. Jesus modeled this. "But Jesus often withdrew to lonely places and prayed." (Luke 5:16)

> *"Jesus often withdrew to lonely places and prayed."*

One of the wonderful benefits of cultivating spiritual disciplines is the growth in self-discipline. Spiritual disciplines that help us to cultivate a relationship with God start with self-control, a fruit of the Spirit. Disciplined coaches and leaders can achieve goals; they are trustworthy and reliable; they have concern for their reputation; and they have the ability to monitor self-behavior. It gets to the issue of motivation, and a motivated person makes for a more effective leader and alongsider coach. "But have nothing to do with worldly fables fit only for old women. On the other hand, discipline yourself for the purpose of godliness; for bodily discipline is only of little profit, but godliness is profitable for all things, since it holds promise for the present life and also for the life to come." (1 Tim. 4:7-8)

I remember the lake's beauty sealing in my mind a wonderful image of God's grace as I rested after a long, dry, hot day of hiking in Wyoming's Wind River Mountains. I was gazing upon a wonderful visual reward after the rugged terrain I had journeyed through. It was an overwhelming scene, and my heart was lifted to a place of praise. Crystal-clear waters reflected the majesty of the surrounding peaks. The fresh mountain air invigorated me, and I breathed deeply of God's creative handiwork.

I observed the special image before me. Freshwater streams, carved into the peaks, fed a high elevation lake in the same way that God's living water flows into the human heart through channels we carve and the ditches we dig by disciplines of the faith. I am learning the value of carving out the tributaries for God's grace and mercy to freely flow.

I also took notice of an upper lake that was smaller and less prominent than the lower, but seemed to have a greater impact on its surroundings. The environment was green, it had abundant vegetation, and its rocky shores provided places for easier access as compared to the lower lake. Even though the lower lake was larger, it didn't have as much impact on its surroundings. Fishing from its cliffs might have been easier, but I am certain that the bigger fish were living in the upper waters.

The upper lake was more appealing because its water was being used. It had a big outlet. Everything going in was flowing out. The beauty was related to closer proximity to the sources of freshwater.

In order for the water to remain clean, pure, and level, there must be an outgoing channel equal to the intake. In God's economy, the outward flow is the reason for the reservoir within and from above. Without it, a thick lagoon of good things turns stagnant.

I wrote some questions in my journal that day. Am I staying close to the source of living water? Am I seeking higher ground in my relationship with God? Do I impact the shores of people's lives who are in my sphere of influence? Am I giving out as much as God is pouring in?

It is for the purpose of this out flowing ministry that the tributaries of grace bring God's fresh and living water into the heart. It flows across the street, throughout our communities and unto the ends of the earth. Life flows to the plains beyond as we walk alongside each other, carving out tributaries with the spiritual disciplines, abiding close to the source of living water. And who knows what weary traveler might see over the rise of a dusty trail to catch a glimpse of abundant life.

Spiritual disciplines cultivate a solid vertical relationship so that the horizontal relationships are supported. The vertical beam of the cross flows to the horizontal, which is about serving people.

Empowered Service

The vertical supports the horizontal. A Christ-centered life marked by love for God flows into love for other people. That means living with a love for others who need the ministry of Jesus in their lives. The reason we serve people is because we have caught God's heart for those who are trying to live without the abundant life available in Christ.

Consider once again the image of what a disciple looks like using the cross. The horizontal beam is really about empowered ministry in the church and outside the church, empowered service in communities of faith and through missional relationships. Christ-centered disciples are passionate about serving in the church. Followers of Jesus are also marked by missional compulsion. For those two wings of serving, the disciple of Jesus is

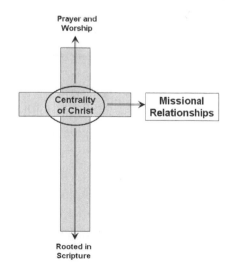

also fully empowered to serve for God's glory. Consider one wing of the horizontal beam, missional relationships.

Devoted disciples of Jesus are missional, which means living out a contagious witness in the context of relationships, meeting people where they are. As McNeal declares, "By identifying, understanding, and meeting the needs of unchurched people, believers live up to their calling to proclaim God's praises for the difference He has made in their lives. Adopting this theological paradigm and ministry philosophy means that the church does not require people to get their act together before coming to God."[40] Disciples of Jesus in our day need to be empowered for a mission mentality. They must be willing to build relationships with pre-Christian people, living and proclaiming truth beyond just protecting it.

I am a fisherman. One of the things that I have discovered is that fish don't just jump into the boat or come swimming up on the shore. There are exceptions of course. Dolphins and whales have been known to beach themselves, and there are stories of fish ending up in a boat when it navigates into a place where a feeding frenzy is happening with fish jumping for insects. In general, however, if a fisherman wants to catch fish he needs to go where the fish are. People need us to step into their lives.

> *If a fisherman wants to catch fish he needs to go where the fish are.*

This will require intentional coaching to improve relational skills. It means learning fishing techniques and learning your best fishing style, figuring out the tools that are in your tackle box and developing your God-given talents and strengths for reaching people. These skills can be learned and improved. Coaching in the context of relationship is a significant training ground for the development of relational skills that will facilitate the ability to be truly missional.

Being missional means a passion for reaching the world. Acts 1:8 becomes a life pattern. Acts 1:8 speaks of power when the Holy Spirit comes upon us. That power is for a purpose, that we can be witnesses. That power for a purpose has a pattern, "…..in Jerusalem, Judea and Samaria, and even to the ends of the earth." Jerusalem is our neighborhood and community. Judea and Samaria are our region. Cross cultural missions is overseas, the ends of the earth, but being truly missional means here, there, and everywhere.

I have become convinced that the most effective witness is a transformed, joy-filled life. People in our world need to see that Jesus is real. He is the King of an eternal kingdom which in one sense is already here but in another sense not yet fully experienced. The abundant kingdom life that people long for is both now and forever. Too often I have been in conversations with people who believe they have secured their eternity but are not living as kingdom people. They have failed to grasp the significance of fruitful and fulfilling life that Jesus has in mind for us now. Jesus calls us to live an abundant life (John 10:10). Alongsider coaching can help people to love, learn, and live in His kingdom now.

With that perspective, aging itself is a process of gaining, not losing, of growing more toward life, not death. That kind of evangelism, lifestyle evangelism, needs to be revitalized. God empowers us to be contagious and finish well. The contagious person longs to hear the words of approval as a servant of the Master. The heavenly kingdom of the future is not just a place to escape this world, but a place that we can begin to live in the light of now. Coaching can help others bring tastes of the kingdom to bear in life today. That is a perspective of kingdom ministry which I believe captures God's heart for people.

Empowered Service in the Church

The other horizontal flow of a follower's cross is toward ministry and service that connects with people in the church, those in the community of faith who are being built up in love, "as each part does its work" (Eph. 4:16). Consider once again the diagram of the disciple's cross:

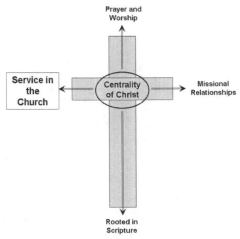

Disciples are active in encouraging others as active participants in the body of Christ. They are team players. That means cooperation rather than competition. Paul said we should all run the race to win, to get the prize (1 Cor. 9:24). However, winning doesn't mean that somebody else must lose. We can all be winners. Running the race to win means we accomplish our goals in Christ and end up winners with other victors on the same team. So much more can be accomplished when we cooperate together rather than compete with each other. Coach Bear Bryant said,

> I'm just a plowhand from Arkansas, but I have learned how to hold a team together—how to lift some men up, how to calm others down, until finally they've got one heartbeat together as a team. There's always just three things I say: "If anything goes bad, I did it. If anything goes semi-good, then we did it. If anything

goes real good, they did it." That's all it takes to get people to win.[41]

What if every person and leader in your church latched on to that attitude? What if we had floods of people willing to live out that attitude as alongsider coaches?

Christ modeled servanthood in leadership, and alongsider coaches must imbed in their hearts the value of serving those they seek to coach. Jesus washed the disciples' feet and He served people in the temple and in the streets. The entire incarnation points to the power of Jesus as expressed in servanthood. Our attitudes are to be the same as that of Christ Jesus, "Who, being in very nature God, did not consider equality with God something to be grasped, but made himself nothing, taking the very nature of a servant, being made in human likeness" (Phil. 2:6-7). Jesus gave it all.

Speaking of giving it all, one of the ways a disciple responds is through giving as an act of worship. That means time, talents, and money. It means tithes and offerings as part of serving the church. It means giving to missional work. Service means more than money, but certainly includes our finances. A good alongsider question might be, "If somebody looked at your checkbook ledger, what would they discover about you?"

Servant leadership runs counter to culture in America, especially in regards to discussions about submission. Yet, a foundational issue for disciple making and leadership development is that if people are going to operate in positions of authority over others, they first need to learn how to submit to authority under others. Helping those we coach to understand the value of submission and servanthood will instill important lessons about God, themselves, and others.

The Service of Learning

Being a participant in community means being teachable. As Schroeder contends, "Teachability is the most basic quality of any disciple and the word 'disciple' literally means 'learner,' and is descriptive of people who are open to new input, not just on the theoretical level but on the practical plane of daily living."[42] Coaches can model a teachable heart and encourage it in the lives of those they are discipling. Being a learner serves others by giving them the opportunity to share a strength and inspiring them to invest themselves in relationships. When you position yourself as a learner, you are not the only one who will benefit.

> *When you position yourself as a learner, you are not the only one who will benefit.*

There must be willingness for Christ-followers to assess themselves and learn from their strengths and mistakes in the context of community. Disciples need to be coached to become comfortable with who they are as God's special children, while being encouraged to allow transformation to place emphasis on who they are becoming in Christ. There is a sense in which alongsider coaches are managers, helping coachees learn to manage their assets and experience the joy of being who God made them to be. Helping people discover who they are and managing their lives accordingly is a significant goal of alongsider coaching. God's work in helping you to understand who you are facilitates effective service and empowered ministry.

Triads

Jesus spent extra time with Peter, James, and John. He took the three of them to the mountain of His transfiguration (Matt. 17:1-2) and to a place of prayer at Gethsemane (Matt. 26:37). Three doorkeepers are mentioned in 2 Kings 25:18 and

Jeremiah 52:24. Moses, Aaron, and Miriam formed an effective triad (Num. 12:4). David was said to have three mighty men, one of whom was named the "chief of the three" (2 Sam. 23:8b). These three mighty men broke through Philistine lines together and drew water from the well near Bethlehem for David (2 Sam. 23:16). Gaius and Aristarchus were Paul's companions (Acts 19:29). In triads we can break enemy lines and draw from the wellspring of God's grace as we walk alongside each other. Coaching triads can be a powerful alongsider strategy.

Discipleship coaching works best in the context of relational community, where there is peer coaching and relationship building that draws out the best in each participant. It might be fitting to call this relational coaching a place of grace, the place where grace is given room, or the "Room of Grace." Bill Thrall, Bruce McNicol, and John Lynch, in their book, *True Faced*, speak about the significant and powerful difference between the "Room of Good Intentions" and the "Room of Grace." The "Room of Good Intentions" is the place of natural religions and institutional structures, the direction that we all tend to drift toward, a place of legalism and a place that allows and encourages the wearing of masks.

The "Room of Grace," on the other hand, is the place of genuine true-faced community where people can mature out of who they really are, a place where people are empowered by the personal work of Christ through the cross. Coaching in a group setting can help to draw out that work and keep people accountable to working out what God is working in (Phil. 2:12-13), being honest about what is going on with the challenges of life.

This relational place of coaching is not a place of mask-wearing perfection but a place where people can be honest and authentic. In this room of grace, alongsider coaches can help others learn to be real and stop hiding. This is an environment where people can reveal what is really true about the sin they have been participants in and victims of. Providing this kind of grace-filled environment is a gift. What a beautiful thing it would be for people to step into places of leadership and service with a genuine understanding of who they are and a feeling of support and community that will keep them in the place of grace, for themselves and to the benefit of others.

It is in the "Room of Grace" where coaching can also extend permission for people to make mistakes and grow from them. One of the greatest gifts we can offer a person we are coaching is a safe place to fail and learn from the experience.[43] That takes some denial of self interests and cross bearing.

> *One of the greatest gifts we can offer a person we are coaching is a safe place to fail and learn from the experience.*

I experienced the joy of a triad on a leadership retreat once. Three of us joined together in prayer and fasting. We also spent time formulating goals in strategic focus areas, seeking God's wisdom in how we can better serve our churches. It was marked by the characterization of a special passage of Scripture, "Speak to one another with psalms, hymns and spiritual songs. Sing and make music in your heart to the Lord, always giving thanks to God the Father for everything, in the name of our Lord Jesus Christ" (Eph. 5:19-20).

At the hosting cabin, there was a clock on the wall with pictures of birds in place of numbered hours. The turn of each hour was announced with the sound of the pictured bird. There was the Bluebird, the Baltimore Oriole, the Kingfisher, a Song Sparrow, a Downy Woodpecker, and a Northern Mockingbird (among others). It was a challenge to guess what kind of bird was whistling its particular tune when the singing alarm interrupted our thoughts each hour. I wondered what they would sound like singing all at once, like a kingdom choir. Would there be conflicting melodies or the blessing of beautiful harmony?

The song of each bird on the clock was unique, much like the tune expressed in the lives of people around us. A triad can offer a three-note chord. I'd like to think that we make beautiful music to God's listening ear as we journey in the unity of Christ in us, the hope of glory. We are not all characterized by the same notes, we aren't heard in the same volume, but there is harmony when we tune in to God's music and capture His conducting heart for our part in His greater song. The unifying rhythm is the missional heartbeat of God for the discipleship of those who follow Him.

It felt to me like the prayers of our little triad were like incense as the songs of our hearts joined together in unison to the glory of God. Sometimes three is better than two, developing a chord of three strands not easily broken (Eccles. 4:12). Triad coaching can leverage relationships toward a great dynamic marked by holy unity and a heavenly bond.

The clock is ticking, God's timing is perfect, and alongsiders share in the hunger for His song to interrupt our wandering thoughts. Coaching helps people stay tuned in to Him. We all know what it's like when people are out of tune. We also long for harmony with others as thankful worshippers of the living God, together in an orchestra of grateful song.

CHAPTER 10

WHAT DOES AN ALONGSIDER COACH LOOK LIKE?

Now faith is being sure of what we hope for and certain of what we do not see. This is what the ancients were commended for. ~Hebrews 11:1-2~

A student fully trained will look like his teacher (Luke 6:40; Matt. 10:24-25). If a coached disciple of Jesus is to look like his coach, there is tremendous value in considering how an alongsider coach can look more and more like Jesus. That means an alongsider coach seeks to be a living example of the previous chapter. This chapter puts some further meat to what it looks like to be a disciple who invests in other people, multiplying kingdom living.

It is a profound responsibility and an amazing privilege to walk alongside other people as you seek to walk more and more deeply with Jesus. As Paul wrote to the Corinthians, "Follow my example, as I follow the example of Christ" (1 Cor. 11:1). We may not like the idea of other people following our example as we follow Christ, but they will. If we are following Jesus, He is making us fishers of men. Somebody in your world is wanting to follow your example. Step alongside them.

Alongsider coaching is also personally satisfying and feeds a sense of purpose and accomplishment in being a part of helping others grow. Whether you like it or not, you are already a role model and perhaps even a hero for someone. Somebody is listening to what you say, watching what you do, and seeking to match up your words with your actions to measure your consistency in service and the life of following Jesus. So, why not step into an alongsider coaching role with intentionality and multiply yourself as you invest in others?

The suggestions of this chapter are simply the rings on a target. God can equip anyone, in the power of His Spirit, rooted in love and relationship, to be an alongsider coach. As Bill Mowry phrases it in his book, *The Ways of the Alongsider* (a tremendous resource and great companion for this book), "God is looking for amateurs to make disciples. This should be an encouragement to anyone wanting to participate in the Great Commission."[44] Andy Stanley's remark in this regard is also helpful, "An effective coach does not need to possess more skills than the person he is coaching."[45] A good coach doesn't need to have all the answers or have it all together, but teachability and willingness to grow and be stretched with others are key marks on the target.

One of the great misconceptions about coaching is thinking that you need to have all the answers to serve as a coach. As Laurie Beth Jones explains in her book, *Jesus Life Coach*, "Coaches don't teach, they facilitate. Coaches don't tell, they draw forth."[46] Coaching isn't about having all the answers, it is about Christ-centered, relational, transformational multiplication.

Walking the Walk

An effective alongsider coach seeks to embody what he or she desires to impart. As the character issues and skills of those we are coaching are considered, coaches must be growing in those arenas themselves. They must also see the value of putting the needs of their coachee first. One of the beauties of this truth is the opportunity to grow with those we are coaching.

A good alongsider coach must be a lifelong learner. Coaching is a learning process and an experience to be shared by both the coach and the

> *A good alongsider coach must be a lifelong learner.*

coachee. Flaherty refers to this as "two tracks" in *Coaching*. Track one is the work that coaches do with those they are coaching. The second track is the ongoing work that coaches must do with themselves in order to stay relevant and effective.[47] Coaches should begin by being coachable and then continue this process by expressing their own self-development to the coachee. This would include being teachable and recognizing that we don't always have the answers. As David E. Schroeder explains in his book, *Follow Me*, "Disciples of Jesus Christ must be readily teachable, even to the point of obeying seemingly absurd commands that violate natural inclinations and cold logic."[48]

Teachability and coachability might include a willingness to learn from the person being coached. As Hicks and Peterson put it, "While you should pursue coaching from many sources, you set a powerful example if you are open to learning from the people you coach. Then, you not only model openness to development, you also strengthen the trust that is so vital to a strong coaching partnership."[49] When a coach is a lifelong learner with a coachable attitude, something contagious can happen in coaching relationships. Umidi summarizes this concept well when he writes, "If you live the lifestyle of a coach—an accountable, authentic, reflective, curious, purposeful life—then your natural life patterns will flow over into the way you coach others. When you do what comes natural to you, you will be coaching. We express this value as 'Ministry flows out of being.'"[50]

An Effective Coach Can Be Trusted

People will not receive your coaching or follow your leadership unless you have taken the time to build their trust. Trust is the only way to get to key character issues which need to become common subjects of discussion. Topics like integrity, sexual temptation, honesty, financial stewardship, arrogance, and relationships are the kinds of issues to talk and pray about in alongsider relationships, and these are matters of character. The only road to approach these topics is through a relationship marked by a bond of trust. Forming a bond of trust isn't complicated, but it must be intentional.

Forming a bond of trust isn't complicated, but it must be intentional.

Trust within a coaching relationship is critical. Sometimes this takes time to develop, and requires an investment of faith and the building of hope in the life of the person we are walking with. Coaches who demonstrate and bring into the coaching relationship both faith and hope working together will help in the growth and development of a faithful follower of Christ. This brings refreshing insights when we read passages like Hebrews 11, known as "the faith chapter." In that context is a list of faithful people who also coached others as faithful servants, building hope and trust that we can emulate.

All of this means that a coach must be moving in the direction of solid character in his or her own life in order to build trust. The prerequisites for church leaders and alongsider coaches in 1 Timothy 3 and 4 and Titus 2 focus on character, not talent or abilities. It is reliable, godly character that is the seedbed for alongside coaching relationships marked by trust.

Listening and Asking Powerful Questions

Effective coaches listen more than they speak. I would suggest that 90 percent of coaching activity is listening rather than speaking. Anderson and Reese write about this as "holy listening." They describe it as "giving attention, developing companionship, enjoying friendship, traveling the road together."[51] This includes sensitivity to the ministry of the Holy Spirit in all places. They also refer to "wholly listening," which involves being fully present, with authenticity, fully aware of the presence of the Holy Spirit. This involves a vulnerability which communicates to others that we are wholly engaged, all of me listening to all of you. Effective coaches will learn the value of both "holy listening" and "wholly listening."

> *Effective coaches will learn the value of both "holy listening" and "wholly listening."*

For true listening to unfold, the first step might be to intentionally let go of your desire to help, motivate, or change the person you are coaching. As a more effective alternative, try to understand that person. Good leaders are good listeners, and great alongsider coaches are great listeners.

In combination with listening, powerful questions need to be utilized. Powerful questions have purpose and relational connection. They are open-ended, like-life. They are more than playing the "twenty-questions" game where you have something in mind and the other person tries to guess what it is. Powerful questions are not rhetorical interrogatives that communicate to the other person that you have something in mind that you want them to say or some defined response that you are looking for. Throwing out questions that communicate your search for a programmed "right" response is torturing with questions, not tutoring with questions.[52] Nobody enjoys playing games by trying to get to "your correct answer." Active listening, becoming okay with silence, and asking powerful questions are critical coaching skills that should be learned and developed. How? Just start doing it.

An Effective Coach Lives In the Present

The abundant life spoken of by Jesus in John chapter ten is for the very present moment. This is a profound truth. The present second is all that we really have. "Now" is all that we can really count on, and getting the fullest sense of life with Jesus in the present is a key profile item for an effective coach. The bottom line is that our only given reality is our situation now. Coaches must live in the present and teach living in the fullness of the moment. When a coachee has the sense that we are fully in the moment with him or her, there is the potential for a deeply connected bond that lends itself to powerful coaching opportunities.

Coaching in this regard can help disciples and emerging workers learn from the past but not be stuck in it. We sometimes miss the joy of the coming moment because we're stuck in a moment behind us. In his book, *Seizing Your Divine Moment*, Erwin McManus writes, "The present moment is where the past and the future collide, and within a moment there is monumental potential."[53] Every moment matters, including the present one and the one to come. This is a message that people need to hear in coaching relationships.

> *Every moment matters, including the present one and the one to come.*

One of the tactics of our enemy is to rob us of the abundant life of the present moment by trying to remind us of past failures or by trying to make us anxious and worried about the future. He is a thief and a robber. Alongsider coaching can team us against his evil strategies.

Coaching can help others discover the joy of the present, breaking out of the crippling effect of being self-absorbed. There is something pure and powerful about the present moment. Effective coaches will help their alongsider friends to be thankful for how God made them in His image, in the fullness of the now, living the abundant life and multiplying it.

Living in the abundance of the present means embracing divine moments. Whether the here and now is an open door, a wall to hurdle, or a narrow hall to negotiate, coaches can help others step forward by faith to get further down the road as they walk alongside on the journey of life.

Living with presence in the present means flexibility. That means that the same coaching questions will not work in all situations. Furthermore, there aren't always easy answers in a coaching situation, and flexibility is an important component of tuning into God's strategy and game plan for the current need. The tools for coaching need to be tailored to fit individual skill levels and needs, driven by the relationship and the needs of the person being coached.[54] Although we often learn the same lessons repeatedly, we should not assume that lessons and strategies of the past will be the same lessons and strategies for today.

A Life Reflecting Missional Purpose

Effective alongsider coaches live with purpose, not by accident. Relationships are important, but in the process they get things done. Purposeful

> *Effective alongsider coaches live with purpose.*

results are informed by both vision and values, which can be developed and encouraged early in a disciple's life. This must be kept in view as coaches work with people on the journey.

Coaches must be missional. One critical character trait of a coach is that of having a heart for the mission of Christ. Church ministry which is missional flows out of an attitude and philosophy of meeting people where they are. For that to happen, there needs to be a shift from a "refuge mentality" to a "mission mentality" in church ministry approaches, along with a shift to a kingdom focus away from "churchianity." McNeal, in his book *Revolution in Leadership*, contends,

By identifying, understanding, and meeting the needs of unchurched people, believers live up to their calling to proclaim God's praises for the difference He has made in their lives. Adopting this theological paradigm and ministry philosophy means that the church does not require that people get their act together before coming to God.[55]

To help someone discover God's best for them requires patience and intentionality. Patience would include giving those we coach the opportunity to try missional endeavors and have the freedom to fail. In fact, the failure rate may be higher for a young disciple whom we are coaching because we encourage him or her to take risks. More risks mean a much higher failure rate. As McManus explains, "It is difficult to fail without risk; it is even more difficult to succeed without failure."[56]

Effective coaches also need to be self-aware in order to live life on mission. Self-awareness enables coaches to be less self-absorbed and more able to help others discover their own strengths and weaknesses in the journey toward a life of purpose. As Christians spend time with God and His Scripture, engage in prayer and worship, walk with a coach, journal, and reflect, they grow in self-awareness for more effective "otherness" and service.

> *Self-awareness enables coaches to be less self-absorbed.*

Consider the example of the apostle Paul. He knew himself well. The book of Second Corinthians gives a glimpse into Paul's own personal understanding. He was aware of his own strengths, weaknesses, passions, and spiritual gifts. Because of that, he had the confidence in Christ and the credibility among the believers to help others. He knew himself well enough to quit thinking about himself and more effectively serve people, becoming a hero of purposeful missional living.

Coaches who live with intentional, purposeful resolve can coach others in the clarification of their goals, the embrace of vision, with reminders of where they are going through prayer and accountability. An effective, sensitive alongsider coach can help people avoid the potholes and obstacles that can slow them down or prevent them from reaching their life and ministry goals. Coaching can also help people get rid of the sins that so easily entangle and slow them down in the race of ministry (Heb. 12:1).

Resourcing

An effective coach is able to resource the coachee. My father worked as a quality control manager for Kelly Springfield Tire Company for years. I learned from my father that quality control means balancing concern about the product with intentional concern for the process. If the process is right, fed by quality resources, product excellence is more likely to be assured. This is also true in coaching and particularly in resourcing coachees for their development and for their approach to challenges. Resourcing them to ensure a healthy process of development is strategic.

One of the ways that coaches can resource coachees is to link them with other people who can help. This means advocating for them in front of others as well as linking them with those who have been in their shoes before or are walking through similar issues currently. Other ways to help resource the coachee would include books, websites, or places to visit, especially the gold mine of the Bible. However, other people with similar stories serve as powerful sources of collaborative coaching as their obedience to the Word of God is given expression.

A significant element of resourcing others is to affirm the value of helping them find the answers themselves and take responsibility for their development. Hicks and Peterson contend, "Coaches don't develop people—they equip people to develop themselves. Rarely will you have the time to involve yourself with every aspect of someone's development."[57] The effective coach will not simply resource the coachee, but will serve as a catalyst for his or her own development. Helping people to become self feeders is indispensable for effective alongsider relationships.

An Effective Coach Is an Encourager and an Advocate

Effective coaches raise up others through encouragement. To develop people you are walking alongside, learn to appreciate them for who they are, believe that they are going to put forth their very best, celebrate their accomplishments, give them the responsibility, hold them accountable, and pray for God's encouragement in their lives.

Alongsider coaches who are encouragers are very motivational. The focus of this inspiration is on action. Motivation serves as the catalyst which inspires a person to act. This means that inspiration and motivation with encouragement is a key tool that should be applied throughout a coaching relationship. This could mean encouraging words, and it could mean the creation of conditions that stimulate the coachee to achieve and perform for God's glory and his or her joy.

One of the unique qualities of a coaching relationship is the flat playing field, equality at the foot of the cross that flows into mutual growth. This means advocating and collaborating, which has to do with working together. In practical terms, this means that the coach is teachable, willing to support the coachee in front of others, and is even willing to encourage a coachee in their advance like Barnabas did for Paul.

Sometimes this means advocating for the coachee when something is not going well for him or her. It might mean doing what you can to obtain for him or her an opportunity for service when others may not be optimistic about a positive outcome. It could include going with the coachee to meet with a person because of tension in a relationship. It always means that we communicate that we believe in them and we believe in a God who is more of an advocate than we could ever imagine.

Encouragement doesn't mean that all coaching dialogues are marked by or limited to praise. Encouragement must include honest feedback, but those conversations can certainly be in the tone of encouragement rather than criticism. In her book, *Coaching and Mentoring for Dummies*, Mary Brounstein writes, "Because constructive feedback is based on observations in specific terms about issues of performance, it is not a right or wrong. Constructive feedback encourages a discussion after the person gets the feedback."[58] Encouraging feedback leads to a positive course of action. To get there, the coach must consider the strategic value of content, manner, timing, and frequency of the feedback given. Encouragement through honest input is biblical and effective.

> *Encouragement must include honest feedback.*

Sounding the Alarm

Enoch was a man who pleased God as he walked with Him (Gen. 5:18-24; Heb. 11:5-6). As Enoch also walked with people, he was known as a man who walked with God. He was a man of prophecy, being able to extend God's warnings (Jude 14-15). These are important components for the profile of an effective alongsider coach. An effective coach knows when to sound the alarm.

Noah, also a man who walked faithfully with God (Gen. 6:9-10), was a man who did everything just as God commanded him and rescued his family (Gen. 6:8-22; Heb. 11:7). He also serves as an example of a godly man who knew how to wave a flag of warning, informing his neighbors of impending judgment (2 Pet. 2:4-5).

Alongsider coaching is not passive. As Brounstein contends, "Being meek,

> *Alongsider coaching is not passive.*

hesitant, indirect, and *laissez-faire* in manner and actions renders coaching useless."[59] There are times when the coach needs to be assertive and "raise the red flag." Listening must be active, asking questions must be intentional, and sometimes there is a need for probing in areas that may not be easy to talk about.

We watched an intense movie recently, called *Unstoppable*. It was about a run-away train that was powered up and running all on its own because of human error leading to an out-of-control situation. The plot revolved around two men who devised a plan to stop the train. They became heroes by putting their train in reverse, hooking onto the run-away train, and putting all the resources of the engines to slow the train down in order to be stopped from derailing on a sharp corner where it would have destroyed itself and many people. Sometimes we need to come alongside people, hook on, and slow them down. Failure to do so might mean they won't make it around the next corner.

Sounding the alarm to stop destructive movement may include confrontation. That can actually be a very good thing. As Maxwell states, "Confrontation, in its best form, is a win-win situation. In this country we have been conditioned to believe that conflict always produces a winner and a loser. But that does not have to be true. To produce a win-win, we must approach confrontation with the right attitude."[60] Jesus was very good at confrontational wins. He often began His coaching opportunities with positive confrontations: "Do you want to be healed?" "Where is your husband?" "Who do you think I am?" Jesus knew that confrontational truth would set people free.

Susan Scott, in her book, *Fierce Conversations*, writes about asking work teams the following question: "On a scale of one to ten, at what level would you like to be confronted— ten being told straight, no holds barred, what someone thinks or feels about something you have said or done?" She noted that most team members would say, "Nine or ten."[61] This provides profound insight that can lend courage to a coach who needs to confront. Most people want to be told the truth in love.

Scott discusses how these kinds of conversations cannot be dependent on how the coachee might respond, and the relationship must be kept at the forefront. She points out that if your life succeeds or fails "one conversation at a time," and if the conversation is the relationship, it is critical to insure that these conversations do take place. In other words, she explains, "If you know something must change, then know that it is 'you' who must change it. Your job is to extend the invitation."[62]

If a well-placed question fails to adequately flag a problem, a more direct approach is warranted. Scott would call this a "fierce conversation." She defines a "fierce conversation" as one "in which we come out from behind ourselves into the conversation and make it real."[63] Effective alongsiding is real, and powerful coaching is happening when an alarm is sounded.

One of the tools suggested by Scott is to replace the word "but" with the word "and" in conversations. In other words, instead of telling the person you are coaching that he or she is working hard at this problem "but" he or she is making some bad choices in the journey, communicate the former with the use of a strategic "and." For example, you might say, "And there are some choices that could be more productive." It is less likely that the person you are coaching will then take a defensive posture.[64]

The raising of the caution flag also means warning those we coach about smaller issues or items of concern that could become problems later even if they are not obvious problems now. Small issues avoided and not acted upon become big issues that have the potential to consume a person down the road. The effective coach can be of great help in this regard.

It seems to be a universal ability, a talent in all of us, to be able to avoid difficult conversations. Knowing when to be direct and issue warnings is a critical coaching skill to be learned and applied. A failure to do so could mean that the very outcomes we fear if we confront someone's behavior now will be almost guaranteed to confront us later if we don't. Then, it may take longer to tackle the issue, and the consequences could show up with the worst timing. There could be a significant price tag attached to problems not addressed as they come up later on in the journey of life.

I used to enjoy the *Bob Newhart Show*. I remember one episode in which he was counseling a woman, informing her there was a time limit and that he would give her two words of counsel. After she told psychologist Bob her issues with open hearted honesty, he summarized his counsel with two words informing her what she needed to do, "Stop it." Those were his two gold nuggets of expensive counsel, repeatedly, after each problem she expressed. "Stop it." She would share her heart, and he would raise his voice each time with his encouragement, "STOP IT." Sometimes the most brilliant thing a person can do is to stop the behavior that has gotten them to the place they are. A good alongsider coach knows when to raise issues of concern to help people choose what is better.

Coaching Landmines

Apprehension to wave the yellow flag or raise the warning banner is a landmine that needs to be avoided. There are appropriate times to call a time-out and address issues of concern that could disqualify a follower of Jesus or take the disciple further down a dangerous road. Future destinations are determined by the present path. Somebody said to me once that you don't need a parachute to skydive. You only need a parachute to skydive twice. If we fail to give warnings, people might never fly again.

There are some other "landmines" to watch for in a coaching relationship, things that could explode to the destruction of the bond of trust, inhibiting the growth of the disciple we are walking with. One of those destructive issues is that of allowing personal issues to cloud the horizon. This is why active listening is an important skill to develop. Failure to jettison the personal agenda in order to provide focused listening can derail a coaching opportunity. Along with this, too much "telling" over "listening" can spoil an alongsider bond.

Another landmine to avoid is neglecting the power of prayer and connection. The two go together, because prayer builds relationship with God as listening and relating builds the coaching connection. Never miss an opportunity to pray. Prayer in itself is a coaching opportunity.

> *Never miss an opportunity to pray. Prayer in itself is a coaching opportunity.*

One of the most dangerous and hurtful landmines is that of a failure to maintain confidences. To share details of a confidential conversation outside the coaching relationship can erode trust and destroy the credibility of the coach. Speaking loosely strips hope, grinds at faith, and is devastating to the trust relationship. A loose tongue can be like an improvised explosive device (an I.E.D.) along the road that can cause pain and destroy the road to healing and growth.

Unclear expectations can be a problem. This can be easily avoided by careful attention to the coaching connection and setting goals in the very beginning. A key ingredient for diffusing this element of danger is communication. Don't ignore the value of clear expectations established at the beginning of a coaching relationship.

Holding on to responsibilities can be problematic. A compassionate, caring alongsider coach must continually be reminded in heart and mind that it is the coachee who is responsible for growth. The coach is not the one on the playing field, but the one encouraging from the sidelines of faith.

Driving back from an event in Butte, Montana, we were the first in a line of cars to be stopped for a towing crew working hard to retrieve a semi truck, tractor and trailer, buried in a ditch full of deep new snow. On a slick road, the trailer had caused the truck to jackknife and set it drastically off course and off the road. I watched the effort, energy, time, and manpower it took to get that vehicle back on the road, holding up traffic for others.

I prayed that God would keep me from ever letting the load of ministry, the burden of work, or the weight of sin that so easily entangles to jackknife me or my family off the path. I resolved to park when needed for a "luggage check" to ensure the presence of the proper goods, throwing off excess baggage. Alongsider coaches watch for sin in their own lives, raise the flag of warning for others, and disarm coaching landmines. The result is freedom in Christ, leading to hope and purpose for a brighter future!

CHAPTER 11

READY, AIM, FIRE

Knowledge is knowing a tomato is a fruit. Wisdom is
not putting it in a fruit salad.
~Anonymous~

It is one thing to know all about a given topic like coaching or disciple-making. Knowledge abounds. The internet can help people discover everything that can be learned about a subject. Wisdom is gaining God's perspective and applying His truth to the circumstances. This chapter is designed to take some of the coaching tools that have been brought forth and help launch you forward in wise use of time for fruitful coaching opportunities.

I have discovered great value in having a simple pattern in mind when walking with other people in alongsider coaching relationships. Like other structures that hold organisms together with all the functions in place, a framework for a coaching relationship has tremendous value when hidden beneath the surface the way a skeleton should be.

I suggest a threefold structure to help keep an alongsider coaching connection flowing with purpose and meaning. The READY stage is marked by getting the relationship readied for coaching to unfold. The second, AIM, is to help the coachee gain focus and clarity regarding his or her life. The third, FIRE, provides impetus for the coachee to take action steps with confidence, hope, and faith. Prayer is the final need before going forth, and that will be covered in the final chapter.

As a former U.S. Marine and as a hunter and rifleman, I relate to a picture regarding everything that leads up to pulling the trigger. Perhaps you have never fired a weapon, but you have certainly squeezed out a decision or aimed at some kind of target with purpose and intent. See if this imagery works for you. If not, think of something that does.

READY

This initial phase of a coaching opportunity scoops up the examples we have already seen in great coaches like Jonathan, Barnabas, and Paul with Timothy. In coaching, relationship is critical. So, the first thing to have in mind is to ready the relationship. That means tuning in first to our relationship with God, which provides the resources for relationship with those we are walking alongside and coaching. When you concern yourself with the fundamentals of your relationship with those you are coaching, you create a foundation for growth and establish the conditions for people to be transformed.[65] Before people are ready to open up, they need to be secure about relational trust.

> *Before people are ready to open up, they need to be secure about relational trust.*

Hicks and Peterson offer great help in this area when they suggest listening to three types of evidence about people's lives and worldviews. First of all, listen to what excites them. Secondly, listen to how they view themselves. Thirdly, listen to what they believe about their ability to develop.[66] Asking relational questions and demonstrating interested listening is the tone of this beginning time of a coaching connection.

To ready the relationship means to continually build trust and avoid that which might derail it. It means building credibility through listening and asking questions, gaining a right to coach. A farming analogy is useful in this regard. First, a person must cultivate the soil of the heart. A lot of time and effort may need to go into readying the relationship in order for the fruit of a crop to grow. This isn't about a linear timeline, however, because there are factors of soil quality and weather that can cause some things to grow at different rates. Circumstances of life can position a person to receive timely coaching outside an agenda.

What does that look like? Do something together. Build relationship. Have a meal. Spend time together in worship and prayer. It is interesting that the day Jesus walked with the disciples toward Emmaus the Scripture says that they recognized Him in the fellowship of food. He was known to them in the breaking of bread (Luke 24:35). Jesus took time to ready their hearts so that out of the relational fellowship their eyes were opened.

I was only six years old and my brother was only four when we nearly burned down the house. We were in the basement earning points with Mom and Dad by cleaning up. We were busy little guys, trying to push around the big broom and moving "stuff" to clean behind. We moved things like a big glass jar that was full of gasoline for the lawnmower. It slipped out of my hands, hit the concrete floor, and shattered. I had two options in my little mind, try to clean it up and hide the damage or go straight upstairs to tell Dad. I didn't know much about gasoline at that point in my life, and so I was unaware of the danger as the gas ran toward the open flame under the old water heater.

Probably with my little brother's encouragement, we ran upstairs to fess up to Dad. By the time Dad headed down the stairs to check out the situation, the flames chased him back upstairs. The whole family quickly abandoned ship, ran over to the neighbors, and called the fire department. The firemen were able to arrive quickly and minimize the damage, and nobody was hurt.

What if I hadn't gone upstairs right away to talk with my father? I was splattered with gas when the jar broke. What if I had tried to cover-up the slip, even if it wasn't really my fault? It was because of a solid relationship of love that had been developed and grown to a place of deep trust that I was ready to run quickly to him. You can be a parent like that, and you can be an alongsider coach like that, helping others to run quickly to the Father because of relationship. They will also come to you for prayer and alongsider encouragement when the relationship is secure.

AIM

Keep in mind that people may approach you for a coaching discussion and want to get right to the key issues they are facing. The very fact that they are getting right to the point might be an affirmation that your time spent in other settings building relationship was effective in setting the stage for helping them to take aim and get to the point they are wrestling with.

Taking aim has to do with life focus. Coaching helps people focus on the right things at the right time. That means carefully zeroing in on where change needs to happen, who one is, and other issues of helping a person get properly centered. These issues, like rings on a target, could be character issues to address, conflicts to resolve, or new ministry opportunities to engage. This is that time in a coaching connection where active listening and powerful questions can help a person take aim on the things that really make a difference. The coach seeks to help the coachee "take aim" by inspiring commitment so that he or she can focus his or her strengths and energies on the things that really matter.[67]

Asking important questions helps people take aim. Where are you? Where do you believe God wants you to be? How might you get there? What are the important issues? What are the obstacles and opportunities? Bill Mowry unpacks this part of coaching in the form of two D's, discovery and discussion. Alongsider coaches help people take aim by helping them to discover truth in the Scriptures and discuss the Word of God together.[68]

An analogy might be helpful. Consider the experiment told of a schoolroom science course. The instructor filled a glass with big rocks and asked if the glass was full. Even though the students were sure that it was indeed full, the teacher then poured in sand to show that more could go into the glass. He asked once again if the glass was full, and the students affirmed that it was, even though they hesitated longer this time. Then, the instructor poured water into the glass to show that more could be put in the container.

The point was that if the water or sand had gone in first, the larger stones would not have gone in. In a coaching relationship there must be a goal of helping the coachee to get the big rocks (the priorities, the things that matter the most) into place in the container of their lives first. To accomplish that is to succeed in aiming at the right things. It includes discovering the solid rocks and gold nuggets that emerge from the Bible.

Taking aim and identifying the big issues doesn't necessarily mean those things are then addressed right away. In fact, I have aimed at a lot of things without pulling the trigger. Sometimes aiming clarifies or even changes the target.

Sometimes in alongsider coaching we need to help people adjust their thinking or refocus their eyes on a clouded perspective. Sometimes that means helping them see that their perceptions or strategies might be wrong. Good coaching means that I don't always just agree with the other person, otherwise we could both be wrong.

Identifying targets and taking aim means getting ready to pull the trigger. It can mean a lot of work and a lot of faith. I love the story of Jocabed and Miriam in Exodus 2:1-9. Leading up to that passage, we know that God was with Joseph and his family and they increased greatly in numbers. The king of Egypt felt threatened by the massive population and strength of this tribe of Israelites. The new Pharaoh was most likely afraid that somebody might go to war with them, then the Israelites would join the enemy and cause defeat from within. He was probably marked by paranoia, jealousy, and fear. So, he appointed taskmasters to impose hard labor.

However, the more they worked the Israelites, the more the slaves multiplied and spread out with their influence. It's funny how that works. The more they were oppressed, the more they grew. When things are at their worst, followers of God are at their best. Coaching somebody in learning how to take aim might mean some level of hardship which brings clarification and advance.

So, the king told the midwives that when they helped the Hebrew women in childbirth they were to put the child to death if it was a boy. That should cut down their population, right? But the midwives "feared God" more than the king. They noticed that these Hebrews had a real, powerful God. As a result, the Israelites grew even mightier and greater in numbers.

Finally, the Pharaoh gave the command that every son born to the Israelites was to be cast into the Nile River. Hundreds of baby boys began to be killed, and the soldiers were involved. Into that setting we find Amram and Jochebed (Exod. 1-2; 6:20). They were Levites, of the priestly family. A son was born to them. What emotions would come into play with the birth of a son under this new Pharaoh who had ordered for every baby boy to be cast into the Nile? Can you imagine what it would have been like to hide a baby for three months in those conditions? Every time he would cry, they would be nervous.

How do you hide a baby? Every time there was a knock at the door, they must have wondered, "Is it the soldiers?"

This mom was determined and committed. Jochebed was a woman who overcame fear by faith. She aimed. She made a plan. She probably spent a great deal of time during those months in prayer, planning, strategizing, considering the big issues and obstacles, figuring out all the scenarios for keeping this baby Moses alive. She watched for possibly significant people who could help and give counsel and prayer support.

Aiming for her meant doing her homework. She knew of Pharaoh's daughter, that the pattern of these ladies was to go down to the Nile for their bath. She knew the current of the river, the right spot to navigate her plan, and probably did several test runs. Then, one day, she pulled the trigger.

FIRE

Jochebed, on a day of great faith, probably with trembling knees, tears running down her cheeks, a huge lump in her throat and a pounding heart, let the baby float out into the Nile River. It was a river full of dangers, including crocodiles and other predators. She must have had some questions. Would her work on the basket fall apart? Would it fail to float? Would it tip over in a current? It was a river where hundreds of babies had already died because of Pharaoh's order. Incidentally, she obeyed the government order, sort of. She floated this fragile work of art out into a river of death, this wonderful baby she had carried for nine months and nursed for three. She released this baby ark out into a dark and dangerous place.

Meanwhile, the sister of Moses, Miriam, was standing in the reeds. She was hiding, watching, and probably praying. She was all part of the plan. She hung out at a distance to see what would happen to her brother Moses. Pharaoh's daughter went down to the Nile to bathe, and her attendants were walking along the river bank. She saw the basket among the reeds and sent her slave girl to get it. She opened it and saw the baby. He was crying, and she felt sorry for him. "This is one of the Hebrew babies," she said.

At just the right, precise, God-inspired moment, with perfect timing (God's timing is incredible and perfect), while Pharaoh's daughter was holding baby Moses, Miriam emerged from her hiding place. She knew that it was up to her to save her brother's life. The pressure was on. She overcame her fears by faith and took an action step.

I'd love to see the video of that scene. Maybe she said something like, "Ooh, isn't he cute, isn't he darling? Wouldn't you love to keep him? He even looks a little like you. Surely he could pass for your very own special son. Shall I go and get a mother from among the Hebrews to nurse the child for you?" All the while she must have been praying, "Help, God!" It was a moment of truth, the trigger has been pulled, would it hit the target? Pharaoh's daughter could just as easily have said, "I must obey my Father and kill the boy."

God blessed the prayers, the readied plans, the aiming strategies, and the action steps of faith. Guess where Moses got to go? He ended up back in the arms of his mom. Pharaoh's daughter said to Miriam, "Take this baby and nurse him for me, and I will pay you." Because Pharaoh's daughter planned to keep the child when he was done nursing, she paid child support! Talk about an outcome beyond what anyone expected, pulling the trigger brought wonderful results that honored God and fed into his plan.

Jochebed never could have dreamed that her plan would turn out so well. She trusted God, floated her dream out into a river of danger, overcame fear by faith, and trusted God for His provision and His promises. What a brilliant plan covered in the tar and pitch of faith.

This is a great picture of a coaching pattern. Alongsider coaches can help a person ready their hearts to hear God's plans and purposes, take aim, weave together a basket of faith, and pull the trigger through action steps that culminate in letting the results be up to Him. Sometimes taking aim means helping people overcome their fears. Being afraid can become crippling if it prevents us from clarifying the issues we need to address in order to get from here to there. It sometimes means releasing faith baskets into uncertain waters, but with the covering of faith great things can happen.

Pulling the trigger means alongsider coaches need to remain in the picture for accountability. Action steps need to be identified and implemented with encouragement coming from the coach. Bill Mowry identifies this as application, accountability, and affirmation.[69] I would hope that Jochebed's husband, Amram, served as an encourager and affirmed her in those action steps of faith.

Clarification of the Target

I learned in the U.S.M.C. that a sniper has to spend a lot of time in readying everything. Equipment must be double-checked. He must be fully prepared and engaged in the mission. All factors must be considered, including distance, wind, weather, moisture levels, type of ammunition, and the mission is always entered into as a team. The process of getting ready and taking aim is a very intentional and detailed procedure of checking all the influencing factors. The target is always confirmed before pulling the trigger. This analogy is helpful for the coaching relationship. The coachee must not pull the trigger on action steps before the necessary work and thought has gone into consideration of all the factors, including identifying targeted action steps.

When aiming a weapon, you hold your breath before pulling the trigger. For the alongsider coach, that means prayer. It means breathing out self and breathing in the Holy Spirit, holding that breath for full empowering, pulling the trigger on action steps and leaving the results in God's hands.

Defining Success

How do you know if the person you are coaching hits the target? It is good to consider what a "win" will look like. Keep in mind, however, that your definition of success might not be the same as God's view of the situation.

On one of my first elk hunts in Montana, I was using a replica fifty caliber black powder rifle. Using that kind of a rifle is challenging. You must insure that the powder is carefully measured into the barrel, that the bullet is properly seated, and that a good firing cap is in place.

It was a very snowy day. On days like that, one must insure that the powder stays dry. I was crouched in almost a sitting position, because I had heard the elk coming. When the large bull elk suddenly appeared and looked right at me, I aimed and squeezed the trigger. Instead of the anticipated explosion of the black powder sending a bullet down the barrel, there was only the unmistakable, disheartening sound of a dry "click." I missed harvesting the trophy bull elk because the black powder was wet.

Even so, success was more about the thrill of the hunt. After pulling the trigger, I had a wonderful experience of finding joy and learning through a mistake. I learned that success might look different after pulling the trigger. The results in ministry are in God's hands, not ours. We may be surprised by what He does in changing the target, even after we have pulled the trigger on a

The results in ministry are in God's hands, not ours.

decision. God has a wonderful way of transforming our understanding of success.

Telling and Offering Advice

When in the course of alongsiding it is appropriate to offer some advice and do some telling, doing so in the firing stage might be tactically profitable. When counsel is to be given, good timing might be experienced when action steps are being identified for pulling the trigger on the right target.

Once the relationship has been readied, aim has been revealed and defined, challenges and issues and problems have been identified, and when solutions have been suggested by the person you are coaching and they have unpacked all they know, the coach can be of great help in encouraging toward action. When all options have been explored together and it is time for taking a step, telling pieces of our own story and offering encouragement and advice are appropriate and strategic.

Soar

When alongsider coaches help others to aim and fire, the result can be launching a person to soar with purpose. Flight on wings like Eagles (Isa. 40) enables discovery of God's renewing strength and power to take them above the circumstances of life, even in weakness.

As an alongsider coach, you might benefit from having this kind of pattern in mind as you walk along with others. It is really quite simple. First is the readying of the relationship and helping a person discover where they are. Then the alongsider coach helps to clear the focus on what the desired future might look like, what God might have in mind for them. That might mean clarifying what success would look like. It might mean helping them to see a character quality or biblical truth by which God is fashioning them to become more fruitful. The alongsider coach can then help a person to pull the trigger on action steps, with accountability. Often, the results of pulling the trigger might look different than expected. It might mean readjusting what success looks like. The results are up to God.

Consider a powerful passage that lifts the heart better than any bullet you could ever pull the trigger on, "He gives strength to the weary and increases the power of the weak. Even youths grow tired and weary, and young men stumble and fall; but those who hope in the Lord will renew their strength. They will soar on wings like eagles; they will run and not grow weary, they will walk and not be faint" (Isa. 40:29-31).

A flock of geese somewhere in the Midwest might serve as a great illustration. These particular geese flew into some very unique weather conditions which caused their wings to ice over, resulting in the geese literally falling from the sky. They could no longer fly. They ran into some inhibiting circumstances which brought them down. It reminded me that I must be alert and careful never to walk into circumstances where God does not want me to be. I must be deliberately in touch with God and walking (even soaring) where He wants me to go, doing that which He desires me to do, remembering the warnings of His word and the example of Jesus in being about the Father's business. That is a secret to spiritual flight, isn't it? Life by the Spirit, keeping in step with the Spirit (Gal. 5). We can't expect His protection and strength when we're not where He wants us to be.

Local volunteers helped the geese to thaw out so that they could fly once again, restored to their former condition of doing what they do so well. God also uses people in His church to gently thaw hearts and restore wings. Warmed and alert to His presence and work around us, we are privileged to experience Him as we seize opportunities to be one of the redemptive volunteers in restoring others. Those opportunities should cause our hearts to soar on eagle's wings. Alongsider coaches have the wonderful privilege of helping people soar to God's glory. Ready, aim, and fire toward a flight path that will hit the right target.

Ready ⟹ Aim ⟹ Fire

*Refresh the Relationships	*Clarify current realities	*Pull trigger on action steps
*Celebrate victories	*Envision desired future	*Encouragement and prayer

CHAPTER 12

ALONGSIDER PRAYER

About eight days after Jesus said this, he took Peter,
John and James with him and went up onto a mountain to
pray. ~Luke 9:28~

This chapter is last with the hope that it will be remembered first. Prayer is essential. It is our first relational responsibility. As John Bunyan explains, "You can do more than pray, after you have prayed, but you cannot do more than pray until you have prayed." One of the most important things coaches can do is pray for and with those they are walking alongside.

I enjoy praying outside, in the beauty of God's creation. I enjoy sitting in the woods by a stream, where worship can be fueled by the wonderful singing of birds. They seem to declare a kingdom song, like the heavens declaring the glory of God, the skies proclaiming the work of his hands, their voice going out into all the earth (Ps. 19:1-4). The birds sing small pleasant songs, recognizable but not overwhelming or overbearing. Like a mustard seed, the smallest known seed to the audience of Jesus when He spoke the words of Luke 13:18-19, "Then Jesus asked, 'What is the kingdom of God like? What shall I compare it to? It is like a mustard seed, which a man took and planted in his garden. It grew and became a tree, and the birds of the air perched in its branches.'" A tiny mustard seed produces the mustard tree, a large herbal plant that grows to be eight to twelve feet tall.

The tree is a place where birds make their nests. It is a place of refuge and protection. When God takes a small faith and produces something big, it can provide peace and refuge. A small seed producing a tree is a powerful illustration of supernatural results from the smallest faith. A sense of hope for others is created. A tree which has grown supernaturally provides a safe haven, a place where songs can be sung. It's a kingdom song, with a rising pitch and increasing tempo.

Supernatural results are produced when we tune in to God's song, even with undersized expressions of faith when we don't feel like singing. It's a song of a growing kingdom. Alongsider coaching moments might be sparked by the tiniest of seeds. Coaching happens when we are tuned in and letting our lives sing with others, recognizing the value of prayer and worship in expressing the language of the soul.

Coaching can be an adventure that involves as little and as much as an individual prayerfully coming alongside another person who needs a friend to walk with during a tough season on the journey of life. Through prayer and other coaching skills, such as good listening and asking powerful questions, coaches can help fellow journeyers to discover God's voice and express God's song in the heart. Through coaching we can help others fine-tune the ability to listen to God's guiding melody.

> *Through coaching we can help others fine-tune the ability to listen to God's guiding melody.*

An effective praying coach can help give voice to the song God is composing and playing in a coachee's life. A coach can help draw out that song so that a coachee is set free to sing God's harmony with his or her very own voice, discovering the joy within through letting God's music ring out as service rings forth. The factor that causes this to happen in spirit and in truth is an abundant life fueled by prayer and worship rooted in God's Word.

Worshipful Prayer

Not all worship happens in orchestrated environments or planned services. I learned this as a dorm parent at Faith Academy in the Philippines. Silence is illusive in a missionary kid boarding home of fourteen. While relaxing in the living room before supper one evening, we began to hear the sounds of kids warming up on their band instruments. Band practice time-sheets were due the next day, and nearly everyone in the dorm was suddenly practicing all at once. Piercing the silence were the guitar and sax, the clarinets and trumpets, a tambourine, keyboard, and a flute. I even imagined a harp in the background. All were resounding at once, different songs to different tempos, striking the ears like a confusing big city traffic jam.

I thought of the closing verses of Psalms, and was reminded that God hears the music of every heart, without confusion. Noise to my ears can be beautiful music when sent forth as a blessing to God. Somehow, He sorts it all out and hears the harmony of all His children singing praise to Him, no matter the tempo or the volume or the notes we play. So, praise Him. Prayer and worship will help you tune in to God and sing His song as a contagious witness. Sing it with others as you walk alongside.

Pray First

I was in a church once where signs were on display everywhere, "Pray First." There was even a "PRAY FIRST" sign in the bathroom. That was a first for me, but a healthy reminder. Prayer should be our first concern, because by prayer we connect with our head coach, our empowering every-present God.

I once heard a missionary tell of how the early African converts to Christianity in a particular area were earnest and regular in prayers and private devotions. They each had separate spots in the thickets near the village where they would pour out their hearts to God. Over time, the paths to these special places of prayer became well worn and could be seen by others. If one of these believers began to neglect his or her prayer times, it was soon apparent to his friends. They would kindly call each other to account, with gentle reminders, "Brother/sister, the grass grows on your path." That sounds like coaching.

This is not to say that prayer should ever become a legalistic activity, but the opposite. Prayer is relational.

Prayer is relational.

Building a relationship takes communication. To neglect communication with God is to allow a weedy invasion. Neglecting prayer also disrupts our relationships with other people. Prayer changes things, that is true. More importantly, however, prayer changes you so that God can use you to help in His transforming work in the lives of people you are walking alongside.

How do people learn to pray? Could a parallel be drawn with how we learned to talk? It had much to do with being around others who spoke. It was rooted in a need to communicate our needs and express our hearts. Even those who cannot communicate with their voices find ways to connect. Our deepest need is to connect and communicate with our Lord. We can coach prayer as we pray.

Prayer is an opportunity to keep God in the center of the coaching relationship. It is an opportunity to focus the relationship through intentional conversations with God, the Head Coach. Prayer doesn't need to be profound or wordy, but it is powerful in keeping God central. Paul writes, "Devote yourselves to prayer, being watchful and thankful. And pray for us, too, that God may open a door for our message, so that we may proclaim the mystery of Christ, for which I am in chains"

(Col. 4:2-3). Devoting ourselves to pray with and for people around us is powerful and contagious.

Warfare Prayer

Those taking up the cross to follow Jesus are soldiers. We are in a spiritual battle. There is a kingdom of darkness and a kingdom of light, and we pray for God's kingdom to come and

> *We are in a spiritual battle.*

God's will to be done. That means we are soldiers in a battle, serving the King. That means our weapons are not the weapons of this world (2 Cor. 10:3-6). It means we keep our armor on together (Eph. 6:10-18). It means prayer as our main weapon.

Kristi and I recently attended a U.S. Army boot camp graduation in Oklahoma, because our son was in the ranks. One of my favorite parts of the ceremony was when all the soldiers, with wonderful unison and enthusiasm, recited the soldier's creed. There was something powerful and inspiring in the demonstrated unity as the soldiers shouted the creed as one voice. Something even more powerful is experienced when people tune in to God's heartbeat and march together in His kingdom rhythm.

Part of the Soldier's Creed was posted in large letters in the auditorium where the graduation took place:

- I will always place the mission first.
- I will never accept defeat.
- I will never quit.
- I will never leave a fallen comrade.

Those words resonate with me as a veteran, but even more as a soldier of the King. Our primary mission is love for the mission giver, with our eyes fixed on Jesus, the author and perfecter of our faith (Heb. 12:2). The deeper life in Him is the wellspring which provides all we need for the mission fields of life and the battlegrounds of faith. The song to which we march is the very heartbeat of our God. "No one serving as a soldier gets involved in civilian affairs—he wants to please his commanding officer" (2 Tim. 2:4).

On days when I have thought about giving up, abiding in Christ is the source of life and strength. When I feel defeated, I choose to walk in victory in Christ. On days when purpose and vision seem foggy, hitting the "refresh" button on the mental desktop with verses like Matthew 28:18-20 helps me stay on track. When others around me are hurting, reaching out to them is part of the honor code as a soldier of Christ. When I feel alone, God reminds me of the plurality in the community of faith.

Warfare necessitates standing in prayer together, because we grow weary in the battle. Have you ever felt alone in the fight? Are there days when the demands of ministry seem overwhelming as the warfare rages around you? We are not alone, and unity toward the mission is a powerful force. As Paul penned it in his epistle to Timothy, "Endure hardship with us like a good soldier of Christ Jesus" (2 Tim. 2:3). Take notice of the words, "with us." Soldiers in alongsider relationships create a powerful army to the glory of God.

Coaching Optimism Through Prayer

A byproduct of the cross-bearing, Christ-centered life is a deep sense of joy, peace, and hope. Disciples of Jesus are marked by a contagious optimism. A result of the Christ-centered life is true joy which develops a hopeful, optimistic outlook on life. We need leaders

> *Disciples of Jesus are marked by a contagious optimism.*

who are inspirational and positive. Most people look for and admire leaders who are honest, forward-looking, and confident about the future. Optimism inspires hope. Credible leaders keep hope alive, they are compassionate, and they reward people. They have compassion, character, competence, and commitment. They are optimistic in a contagious way as they pray.

My younger son and I broke down in a Louisiana rainstorm with an old van he had purchased. As we gazed at the engine, we could see that several important hoses had come apart and steam was rising from everywhere. We were standing in a torrential rainstorm. It was raining so hard that we were soaked within seconds. We were hundreds of miles from home. Things couldn't get much worse. I looked at the steaming engine, feeling cold and wet, very tired after a long drive to pick up the vehicle, with no idea what to do next. I shifted my gaze to my son standing next to me. He was smiling.

When I asked him how he could manage a smile in this situation, he reminded me that he had recently returned home from service in the U.S.M.C after tours in both Afghanistan and Iraq. "This is nothing, Dad." He changed my perspective and enabled me to shift my inner prayers to a more hopeful posture. He is an optimist.

A search for "optimism" in the Bible will yield no results. There are plenty of studies, however, on words like "joy," "rejoicing," "faith," "peace," "confidence," and "hope." These terms are found together in Scripture, and these are qualities which coaches build into others when they approach life with prayerful optimism.

Optimism, like faith and hope, does not mean simply waiting for good things to happen. It may not be easy to clearly define or prescribe on paper, but you know it when you see it. A great artist was once asked, "What's the best picture you've ever painted?" "The next one," he replied confidently.

The Bible proverb, "A merry heart doeth good like a medicine" (Prov. 17:22), has good logic in it. The healing beams of sunshine in a Christian's hope sustain an optimistic glow. Jesus said that we would have trouble, but we are to take heart that He has overcome the world (John 16:33). Leaders must believe and walk intentionally in joyful, optimistic truth.

A sense of humor helps. Sometimes we take ourselves too seriously. This is more than just being able to tell a good joke. It has to do with being able to find joy in any situation, finding the humor in moments of inadequacy.

> *Sometimes we take ourselves too seriously.*

This doesn't mean sarcasm or inappropriate laughter that reveals social awkwardness, but simply the ability to tap into that peace of God which enables laughter to flow with genuine and authentic joy. Your smile might be one of the most powerful coaching assets you have. I hope there are times that you smile during prayer.

Learn to laugh at yourself. I remember a time on vacation, when I was just a kid, that I took a canoe out on the lake where we were staying at a cabin. My family members were all standing on the shore, so I stood up in the canoe to wave at them. In the process, I fell right out of the boat. Getting back in was not easy, but the process caused me to laugh out loud at the whole experience, knowing that it must have looked very funny to those on shore. My uncle said that was the day I grew up.

People like to follow joyful, optimistic people. Life is really more about attitude than circumstances. The perception of an event can be more harmful than the experience. Interpretation of experiences and the responses to them can be coached by the alongsider.

> *The perception of an event can be more harmful than the experience.*

Optimism is essential, and it often comes down to a choice to rejoice. Paul wrote to the Philippians, "Do everything without complaining or arguing" (Phil. 2:14). He also said, "Rejoice in the Lord always. I will say it again: Rejoice! Let your gentleness be evident to all. The Lord is near. Do not be anxious about anything, but in everything, by prayer and

petition, with thanksgiving, present your requests to God"
(Phil. 4:4-6).

This means refusing, by faith, to embrace negative thinking
that can bite us. Consider these words by Laurie Beth Jones:

> Once I had a dream where I was wading in a river
> full of snakes floating by me. I made it to the other side
> by not panicking and certainly by not picking up any
> of the snakes. Negative thoughts are like snakes. If you
> let them float past you, you'll be okay. But if you grab
> them and try to wrestle with them, you're in for some
> fang time.[70]

Have you had any fang time lately? Fang time used to
hit me every Sunday afternoon when I would overanalyze a
sermon I had delivered, a Sunday school lesson I taught, or a
worship service I led. If you are a task-oriented person, it can
be far too easy to become performance based and dwelling on
less than perfect outcomes can be a joy robber. Developing the
negatives can be a dark room in need of enlightened optimism
by leaving the results up to God and praying both when things
are going well and not so well.

I like the words of 1 John 1:4: "These things we write,
so that our joy may be made complete." Telling, writing,
and prayer journaling can be transformative in this regard.
Memorizing Scripture can also be a powerful tool for building
optimism and hope. Read more Scripture. Pray more. Smile
more. Let your heart sing.

Praise and Celebration Prayer

In terms of coaching, every prayer should include some
element of praise and celebration unto God. It builds hope
and faith. As James Nicodem states it in his book, *Prayer
Coach*, "Happiness should not go unexpressed. It must be
given voice. And the One to whom we address these outbursts,

first and foremost, should be God."[71] There are many biblical examples of people celebrating, praying, and worshiping after great things happened. Jesus modeled it. After calling the first disciples and healing the man with leprosy, the news about Jesus spread all the more and many came to be healed. Ministry was great, everything was going well. Notice how Jesus handled success. "But Jesus often withdrew to lonely places and prayed" (Luke 5:16). When things are going well, don't miss an opportunity to celebrate with the Father! When there is something to be happy about, we must be quick to communicate our joy to the source of joy and victory. Coaches are wise to find reasons for celebratory prayer.

Praise and celebration in our prayers isn't always fueled by what is happening around us. For example, why is it that the evening news usually starts with the introduction, "Good evening," and then the reporting convinces you that the world did not have a good day? How can that encourage a good evening?

Alongsider coaches should seize opportunities to praise God. Philippians 4:4 commands us to rejoice in the Lord always. The Lord 's Prayer (or

Seize opportunities to praise God.

perhaps better named the disciple's prayer) sets a pattern for prayer to begin and end with hallowing, honoring, and praising God. Colossians 4:2 says, "Devote yourselves to prayer, being watchful and thankful." First Thessalonians 5:16-18 commands us to be joyful always, praying continually, giving thanks in all circumstances, for this is God's will for us in Christ Jesus. It fills the heart to express gratitude to God, and encourages the people we are coaching. There is always something that can be celebrated.

Redemptive Prayer

During a short-term mission trip to a Bible camp in Rio Chico, Mexico, one of the tasks I took on was to clean out and sort the tool storage room. The area was quite a mess, loaded with things deposited and stored, full of cobwebs and dust. It was a challenge to decide what to keep and what to toss as I took on the badly needed project. The culturally appropriate thing to do would be to save everything.

I took many items of "junk" that weren't quite ready to put in the garbage can and threw them into an assorted miscellaneous box. I like those kinds of boxes, where you store all kinds of odds and ends that you might need someday. You would probably need the thing moments after you pitched it, so you keep it just in case. Many of the items become forgotten until you dig through that junk drawer the next time. Do you have one of those places?

As I wondered what to do with some old rusty metal parts, I thought about those things from my past that are like corroded pieces of metal I'd rather not remember or see again. Like old stiff paintbrushes that might represent the false pictures people painted of me by saying things that weren't true. It hurts when you are misunderstood and misrepresented. Or, maybe it's old rusty nails, like the hurtful sharp things people have said to you. Redemptive prayer includes forgiveness. Perhaps you have memories of being taken advantage of, abused like an old plumbing fixture. What about the time you said or did something you wish you could take back, like an old vacuum accessory buried with other junk?

I think there must be some kind of shelf in my heart for all of those miscellaneous things of the past. Perhaps it's wise to just hang on to them and leave them in an assorted box, trusting God to use them for some good purpose or to help shape me to be more like Jesus.

In the United States, we too quickly throw everything away when we clean house. Maybe it's wise to just shelf some things that we would rather forget and toss. If God wants to rebuild something or pull it off the shelf to work for the good in me and through me, great. Maybe it was some hurt or moment of pain or suffering like a piece of rusty plumbing. Maybe God will want to pull that off the shelf someday and use me as a channel of living water to bring refreshment to a hurting soul. Maybe it's an extra piece of wiring or an electric fixture that God may want to drag up and use to bring faith and power to someone in a time of weakness or darkness. Perhaps an old rusty nail can be pulled out of the miscellaneous drawer of my heart and be straightened and used to hold some relationship together.

Redemption is so sweet. God can take the junk from the past and sanctify it for kingdom work, and prayer is the workbench altar. Alongsider coaches must be people of prayer, inviting God's work in

> *God can take the junk from the past and sanctify it for kingdom work.*

their lives and in the lives of people they are walking alongside, no matter what old tool God wants to use.

Staying Power

Alongsider coaching with prayer can help disciples stay on the playing field of life and maintain focus on Christ and mission. Coaching is a key component of helping people finish well. It is the secret weapon for sticking to it and making a fulfilling impact. Staying power is modeled by the faithfulness of Jesus, who, "…for the joy set before Him endured the cross" (Heb. 11:6). The greatest reward is God himself, who promises to be with us always (Matt. 28:20). Coaches help people stay the course by the reminder

> *Coaches help people stay the course.*

that God sticks with us and will never leave us or forsake us (Deut. 31:8).

A good friend of mine is a competition trap and skeet shooter. He was a great coach when I first took up the sport. He shared with me one of his experiences in a competition. Nearing the end of the shoot, he was in the lead and had essentially won. He only had one more round to top off his winning score. He explained how his heart was already set on the big win. He was already mentally signing his name on the trophy as he entered the final round. Then he missed. He ended up not winning because in his heart he had left the field early. This is an athletic principle that we can all learn from: never leave the field before the game is over. Never leave the task unfinished. Don't start the final play without a heart fully engaged in the present moment.

Alongsider coaches can help people learn this principle in their daily journey with Jesus Christ. The enemy of our souls comes as a thief (John 10:10). He is good at reminding us of our past or seeding our hearts with anxiety or false expectations about the future. Living in the past or the future can cause us to leave the field, even if only in the thought life. Jesus came to give life, and life more abundantly, life in the present moment. Are you fully engaged in the kingdom task which God has set in your heart for today? Are you living in the abundance of the present moment? The "right now" is what really counts. Coach that.

Alongsider Prayer Targets

Remember that the two key components of effective coaching are active listening and asking powerful, open-ended questions. Prayer is essential, both for people we are coaching and with them. This helps to cultivate listening with a third ear to the voice of the Holy Spirit. Meeting on a regular basis is strategic, because cultivating the relationship is foundational. In those coaching connections, be deliberate in planning to meet and allow a format that is informal and safe, where accountability and spiritual sharpening can occur.

Always keep the end product in view, remembering that raising kids, releasing disciples, and sending emerging workers to meet the needs of the harvest is the culmination of coaching. That means resourcing them and helping them to unpack all the assets within their reach. Remember that the one being coached needs to do the work to accomplish lasting growth.

Be aware of opportunities to give people the freedom to fail. The only people who never fail are those who never try anything. Effective coaches advocate for those they are coaching, providing practical opportunities for them to try new things, discover what their strengths are, and be able to learn from their mistakes.

> *The only people who never fail are those who never try anything.*

Be a lifelong learner yourself, and be vulnerable. Be open and real about your own spiritual journey, sharing your struggles and failures as well as the positive successes. An open life of integrity which starts from the example of a coach living in full dependence on God is powerful and effective. Tell your story but give advice sparingly.

People need others to coach them toward reaching their maximum potential and make their maximum impact for God in a way that brings true joy and fulfillment. To become all that we can become in Christ and in service to God, we need people walking alongside us in coaching relationships. Without these kinds of relationships it is not possible to become all that you have the potential to become.

This book was written from the perspective of a Christ follower who is walking with Jesus alongside others. If you are following Jesus, you definitely, assuredly have something to give. You have much to offer. True alongsiding is about being an instrument of true encouragement for others, helping them to be all they can be.

Jesus said, "Apart from me you can do nothing" (John 15:5). With Jesus comes purpose, meaning, and the fulfilling sense that you can have a positive influence on people in your world. If you are not a Christian, be encouraged to consider the life and purpose He offers. Before I became a follower of Jesus, I was usually on empty walks. Once I began to follow Jesus, I discovered amazing grace, mysterious love, and a fulfilling reason to live. As I learned to walk with Him alongside, I began to understand walking alongside others. May I encourage you to walk with Him alongside people He has already put in your path.

As alongsider coaching relationships unfold and progress, always find reasons to celebrate. Abundant life with Jesus is an exciting adventure. Watch for opportunities to encourage faith-filled risk taking.

> *Always find reasons to celebrate.*

As I finish up this book, I'm remembering a moment a few days ago with my older son. He was talking about future dreams. In a fun moment, he fired up a Bic lighter several times. I leaned toward him and blew it out. We had a moment of eye contact where both of us understood a point. Don't blow out the flames of a person's dreams. Fan the flames carefully so that they don't get extinguished. Alongsider coaching can help people become all that they can become in Christ in order to make their maximum impact unto His eternal glory.

After Jesus left those two disciples He had walked with on the Emmaus road, they asked each other, "Were not our hearts burning within us while he talked with us on the road and opened the Scriptures to us?" (Luke 24:32). That is what alongsider coaching can do, fuel hearts with a burning passion for Jesus.

Appendix

Powerful Questions of Jesus:

- "What is written in the Law? How do you read it?" (Luke 10:26)
- "When I sent you without purse, bag or sandals, did you lack anything?" (Luke 22:35)
- "What are you discussing together as you walk along?" (Luke 24:17)
- "Why are you troubled, and why do doubts rise in your minds?" (Luke 24:38)
- "Do you have anything here to eat?" (Luke 24:41)
- "What do you want?" (John 1:38)
- "Where shall we buy bread for these people to eat?" (John 6:5)
- "Where are they? Has no one condemned you?" (John 8:10)
- "Do you believe this?" (John 11:26:b)
- "Will you really lay down your life for me?" (John 13:38a)
- "Is that your own idea, or did others talk to you about me?" (John 18:34)
- "Friends, haven't you any fish?" (John 21:5)
- "Simon, son of John, do you truly love me?" (John 21:16)
- "Why are you talking about having no bread? Do you still not see or understand? Are your hearts hardened? Do you have eyes but fail to see, and ears but fail to hear? And don't you remember? When I broke the five loaves for the five thousand, how many basketfuls and pieces did you pick up?" (Mark 8:17-19)
- "But what about you? Who do you say I am?" (Mark 9:29)

READY

Questions to help ready and establish the coaching relationship:

- How does the world look to you these days?
- What are you most passionate about these days?
- What are you doing for fun?
- Tell me about the last good laugh you had.
- What makes you laugh?
- On a scale of 1-10, what is your level of optimism?
- Who in the Bible would you like to be coached by and why?
- Who has been a significant coach for you in the past?
- Talk about the last time you had opportunity to coach someone on the issue of God's will, His calling, or His purpose. What passages of Scripture have been important for you in that regard?
- What is your favorite time of day?
- What is your favorite season?
- How has someone helped you be conscious of the Holy Spirit's work when you were making a decision?
- How can planning in a coaching relationship provide and promote freedom?
- What example could you give of being guided by the Spirit in a time of planning, preparing, or goal setting?
- How do you balance family and friends?
- If you were going to write a book about relationships, what would you call it?
- Who engages you most readily in conversation?
- What five accomplishments are you most proud of?
- What do you do when you are bored?
- What does the love of God mean to you?
- Who has most modeled God's love to you?
- What did you like about the town you grew up in?
- What is your fondest memory of childhood?
- What is your worst memory of childhood?
- Are you a news-watcher or a news-maker?
- If you were a candy bar, what kind would you be? Why?
- What's the best practical joke you've ever pulled?
- What is helping you to have a positive attitude these days?
- How is God expressing His love for you?

AIM

Questions Concerning Life

- What does the word "optimism" mean to you?
- As you consider what you are most passionate about these days, how is that connected with your passion for God?
- Is anything heavy on your shoulders these days?
- What are the key passages that might offer encouragement in your relationship with the Father?
- What are you doing to cultivate your love relationship with the Father?
- What might be a good book of the Bible to read to refresh the idea of cultivating love for God and living a great commandment lifestyle?
- Who else might you network with who could help you to cultivate an intimate love relationship with God?
- Who in your world models a love relationship with God?
- Who do you need to spend some time with?
- What resources do you have already that might be helpful?
- What are your greatest challenges these days?
- What is the most challenging area of your life that is in need of self-control?
- If you could do it over again, what would you do differently?
- How might self discipline help in the fulfillment of your life purpose?
- What decision have you been avoiding?
- Where have you been asleep at the wheel?
- What are the most effective spiritual disciplines for you?
- Who is the most self-disciplined person you know? What about that person could you apply to your own life?
- Give me some reasons why optimism might be important as a leader.
- Is anything heavy on your shoulders these days that might be robbing you of joy?
- What key passages of Scripture is God using in your life?
- If you were to teach people how to have fun, what would you say?
- If there were a "dark side" to optimism, what would that be?
- What are some key passages that might offer insights into cultivating optimism?

- What are you doing to cultivate your love relationship with the Father for the building of faith?
- Tell me some more about _____. What was fun about it?
- When you are ninety-five years old, what will you want to say about your life?
- What is the most joyful thing that could happen in your life this week?
- Who could you get to play with you on a project or activity?
- What is the most important thing you and I should be talking about?
- How do you balance work and play?
- How do you balance strengths and weaknesses?
- How do you balance the realities of life, both professional and social?
- How do you balance emotional, physical, and spiritual needs?
- How important is balance?
- What are the core values of your life?
- Are you missing anything of importance in your life?

Questions about Change

- How does change happen in your life?
- Where are you taking your foot off the gas?
- How are you doing with _____ (anything that may have been a distraction in cultivating of an optimistic attitude)?
- If we could wipe the slate clean, what would you do next?
- Where might you be in denial?
- Could we explore _____ further?
- What needs to change if you are to become more optimistic?
- What might we be able to celebrate the next time we meet?
- What kind of change do you face most calmly?
- What kind of change is most emotional for you?
- How have you changed for the better? For the worse?
- What questions might you ask yourself each morning?
- What can I do to help you?
- Who else might you network with who seems to have a high level of optimism and joy?
- Could we brainstorm this issue?

- How balanced is your life right now?
- Do you change or do things change around you?
- What person has most helped you change for the better?
- Where are you procrastinating? What are you avoiding that you know needs to be done?
- If you could ask anyone three questions and have guaranteed honest responses, whom would you question and what would you ask?
- What are the people around you pretending not to know?
- What are you pretending not to know or reveal about yourself?
- What seems impossible that if it *were* possible it would change everything?

Questions about Who You Are

- What is the most significant thing that has happened since the last time we met?
- What are your regrets?
- What patterns in your life might be significant in how you have been shaped?
- If the focus of your life were banking happy memories and fulfilling relationships, how rich are you?
- If you could create the absolute perfect job for yourself, what would it be?
- What would you wish for your children?
- Are you a cat person or dog person?
- If you could accomplish one crazy stunt that would put you in the *Guinness Book of World Records*, what would it be?
- If your name were to appear in the dictionary, how would you define yourself?
- How are you just like your father? Your mother?
- What makes you feel the most vulnerable?
- When do you feel the most fully engaged in living?
- What would you like to learn how to do?
- What three nouns best describe you? Adjectives?
- What's the funniest thing that has ever happened to you?
- When have you been doubled over with laughter?
- If you could become one historical figure, who would it be? Would you change anything about how he/she lived his/her life?

- What was your favorite toy when you were young?
- Did you ever have a nickname? What did you like about it?
- What animal would you like to be? Why?
- You are asked to create one new national holiday, what would you call it? What would it celebrate and when would it be?
- What if God wanted an even dozen commandments instead of ten, what might the additional two be?
- If you were a member of the opposite sex, what would your name be?
- When do you feel most creative?
- If you had just one more day to live, what would you do? Six months?
- If you could change one decision you've made in your life, what would it be?
- What is your definition of "rich"?
- Your favorite singer is writing a song about you. What's the title of the song? Sing it.
- If you had one extra hour each day, what would you do with it?
- If you had one extra day each week, what would you do with it?
- Who are the three greatest people in history?
- If you were President of the United States of America, what's the first thing you would do?
- What do you feel is your life's central emotional challenge?
- What would you like to say to your father but just haven't been able to say?
- Have you ever said anything that you wish you could take back?
- What gift has God put in you that He has developed over time?
- What gift has God given you that you are not able to use right now?
- What was your best subject in grade school? High school? College?
- Who was your best teacher? What did he or she teach you?
- Which would you rather explore: outer space, the ocean depths, or the Yukon?
- What do you carry in your pockets? In your briefcase or backpack?

- What is the single most expensive item you own?
- What are the three greatest inventions of all time?
- A new TV sitcom is going to be created, based on your life. What is the name of the show? Describe the major characters. What is the basic plot?
- The TV show *60 Minutes* is going to do an exposé on you. What skeletons have they discovered in your closet? How will you respond?
- Who is your hero?
- If you could change one of the Laws of Physics, which one would it be? What would the new law be?
- If you could live in the past, what year would you go to, and what location would you go to?
- If you could live in the future, what year would you go to, and what location would you go to?
- What old stories from your life do you drag along with you?
- If you had been the first person on the Moon, what would you have said as you stepped onto the surface?
- If you could save just one object from your burning home, what would it be?
- If there were eight days in a week, what would you do with that extra day?
- What is your greatest strength?
- What would it be like to live out your strengths every day?

FIRE

- Where do you need to act?
- What Scriptures might be good to memorize and hide in your heart?
- What do you sense you need to do now?
- What needs to change if you are to grow in your love for God?
- What might we be able to celebrate the next time we meet?
- What other angles can you think of?
- What do you want to be remembered for?
- Where do you need to wait for God to act?
- What opportunities are confusing you right now?

- Of the specific choices that you are facing, which of those fits your personal mission?
- What would it look like to be handed a new script for the play of your life today?
- Of the ideas we have discussed, which one has the greatest potential for future success?
- What will you take away from this time?
- How can we lock in a learning strategy?
- What kind of plan do you need to create?
- What are some of the obstacles that keep you from a deeper prayer life?

Missional Questions

- What are your spiritual beliefs? What does the word "faith" mean to you?
- What does the term "Christian" mean to you?
- Why do you think you are here on earth?
- Do you believe there is a Creator?
- If you do believe that there is a Creator, should He have any input into your life?
- Do you ever read the Bible?
- Tell me about the most joyful experience of your life. Is there any chance that God was involved?
- What has been the greatest challenge you have faced? How did you get through it?
- If you were to die today, do you know what would be next?
- Do you believe in heaven and hell?
- Have you ever needed to forgive someone?
- Have you ever needed to forgive yourself?
- Do you think God cares about forgiveness?
- If Jesus were standing before you and said, "Come, follow me," what would hold you back?
- Are you happy with the direction of your life right now?
- What gets you up in the morning?
- If you had to pick a hero, who would that be? Why?
- Why do you think that people struggle with believing that Jesus is God?
- Why do you think Jesus died on a cross?
- Would you ever use the word "sin?" If so, How?
- When random shootings occur where innocent people are killed, is there sin involved? According to whom?
- What do you think the standard is for getting into heaven?
- To you, who is Jesus Christ?
- What do you think is the primary reason Jesus came to earth?
- What do you think a personal relationship with God looks like?
- You have children. What—if anything—are you teaching them about God?
- If you could ask God any questions, what would they be?
- In my religious world, we classify people as "believers" (part of the Christian community) or "seekers" (people on a search for spirituality and God). How would you classify your own spirituality?

- There is a great emphasis these days on prayer. To you, what does it look like to pray?
- If you were wrong about any of your spiritual beliefs, would you want to know it?
- What would your level of interest be in finding answers in the Bible?
- How can I pray for you?

Discussion Guide

CHAPTER ONE

Discussion and Reflection

1. Read Acts 2:14-21. When Peter stood up to preach (2:14), who was alongside?
2. What are some of the "grains" God created in you? What does it look like to be grateful for the way God made you?
3. What tool is God using on the workbench of your life? How is He shaping you?
4. How would you define coaching?
5. What are some of the key benefits of coaching, both to you and to those you coach?
6. What inhibits some people from a willingness to coach others?
7. What are you learning about yourself?

Alongsider Coaching Challenges

- Identify at least two people who could benefit from an alongsider coaching relationship and ask if they are interested. Explain that you are sharpening your coaching skills as you read this book and that you would like to come alongside them.
- Come up with a set of questions that will help the people you are coaching to discover something new about God's "grain" in their lives, how he wired them and made them the way they are today.

—٨٨١—

CHAPTER TWO

Discussion and Reflection

1. How is your relationship with God?
2. What trail are you blazing for others to follow?
3. What legacy would you like to leave behind?
4. Where are you going these days in your journey with Jesus? Who is walking with you?
5. Which of your favorite Bible characters would be good alongsider coaches? Why?
6. What is a powerful question that someone asked you recently?
7. Hebrews 4:12 speaks of the Bible as a sharp, double-edged sword. What Bible passage is God using to sharpen you?

Alongsider Coaching Challenges

- Do a Bible study on your favorite hero from the Bible and share with someone, maybe the person you are coaching, why that hero would make a great alongsider coach.
- Share something God is teaching you about your journey.

—⁓—

CHAPTER THREE

Discussion and Reflection

1. Read Matthew 22:34-40. What is the greatest commandment? Why should we obey? Consider John 14:15-23.
2. What hinders your ability to love others?
3. Who are your closest fellow soldiers? Talk about a recent battle you fought together that enabled you to sharpen each other. "As iron sharpens iron, so one man

sharpens another" (Prov. 27:17). That includes women sharpening women, young adults helping each other, and children learning the art of relationship.

4. Who has walked alongside you in the past? Thank God for them. Perhaps that means thanking God by thanking them.

5. What is the difference between independence and interdependence? Between uniformity and unity?

6. What impresses you the most about the relationship between Jonathan and David? Talk about a coaching or mentoring relationship you have experienced that was similar to what Jonathan and David had.

7. What conversation are you avoiding?

Alongsider Coaching Challenges

- Jesus said that if we love Him we will obey Him (John 14:15, 23; 15:10). One profound way to express love for God is through obedience. An obedience test is a love test. Are there any people in your life who might serve as an obedience test, an opportunity to love God by loving them? Walk alongside them for a season.

- Read through 1 Corinthians 13 with someone and talk about what love looks like in an alongsider relationship. Talk about boundaries that should be in place in order to embrace the paradox of interdependent independence.

—₥—

CHAPTER FOUR

Discussion and Reflection

1. What are the competing voices you battle? Counsel from the wrong people? A boss who fails to have your best interest in mind? Too much "noise"?

2. Read James 1:19-21. Describe a time in your life when you were listening to the wrong voices and spoke too quickly.
3. Discuss this quote by Dallas Willard: "Hearing God cannot be a reliable and intelligible fact of life except when we see His speaking as one aspect of His presence with us, of His life in us. Only our communion with God provides the appropriate context for communications between us and Him. And within those communications, guidance will be given in a manner suitable to our particular lives and circumstances."[72]
4. What does "listening physically" look like to you? Who has modeled that for you?
5. Have you ever found yourself on a mental trail and discovered suddenly that you weren't really listening to the person talking with you? Talk about that experience.
6. Talk about the last time someone gave you the gift of listening.
7. Read 1 John 4:4-12. What does this passage teach about listening? What does love have to do with it?

Alongsider Coaching Challenges

• Consider starting a prayer journal page or a coaching log to jot down key items of prayer on behalf of those you are coaching and walking alongside.
• Try cultivating a listening heart in your own devotional times with God.

—∞—

CHAPTER FIVE

Discussion and Reflection

1. Where are you, really?
2. What are the most significant questions you have heard or been asked?

3. Read Revelation 5:1-2. In what way is the question of the angel a proclamation?
4. What do you want Jesus to do for you today? What do you believe is God's desire for you?
5. What are you seeking? What are you hungry for? Where do you want to be?
6. What are some bad "why" questions? What "why" questions might be good?
7. What sin makes you angry?

Alongsider Coaching Challenges

- Start developing your own list of powerful questions.
- Consider the questions in the appendix and make a list of your favorites. Try a few questions on people around you this week, and listen well.

—∞—

CHAPTER SIX

Discussion and Reflection

1. Talk about the last time you found yourself in an unexpected place. What did God teach you?
2. Tell about the last opportunity you had to share your faith or have a spiritual conversation with someone who is not following Jesus.
3. Read 1 Peter 2:21. What is God calling you to?
4. What "territory" have you taken?
5. What are some of the obstacles to a creating a coaching culture in your church?
6. What are you willing to risk?
7. Who are you investing in?

Alongsider Coaching Challenges

- Watch for someone who is in a season of difficulty and

pray for God to provide an alongsider for them.
- Establish some achievable goals in your coaching relationships. Encourage the person you are coaching to do the same with someone else.

CHAPTER SEVEN

Discussion and Reflection

1. Talk about the last time you had the opportunity to share the hope you have in Jesus.
2. Read Philemon verse 6. What is the connection between sharing faith in partnership with others and getting to know Jesus better?
3. What does it mean to be a team player?
4. What are your favorite questions for sharing your faith?
5. Who are the "big fish" for whom you need to pray?
6. What is your favorite "fishing bait?" What Bible passages have you found effective for witnessing?
7. What fear holds you back from sharing your faith?

Alongsider Coaching Challenges

- Be encouraged to develop a list of questions that might help you to embrace opportunities to share your faith through alongsider coaching relationships. Pick one. Go ask it.
- On a sheet of paper, make a list of the fears you have. Read Philippians 4:6 and pray over your list. Hear the words, "Do not be afraid." That is a command. Make a decision to obey it and throw your list away.

CHAPTER EIGHT

Discussion and Reflection

1. Read Matthew 16:24-26. What does it mean to deny yourself and take up your cross to follow Him?
2. What is it to surrender?
3. What would free you up if you left it at the foot of the cross?
4. What makes you laugh?
5. What is God teaching you about your weaknesses?
6. What are your strengths?
7. What is God calling you to do next? With whom?

Alongsider Coaching Challenges

- Help the people you are coaching to step out in faith and try something new in serving God.
- Step out and try something new yourself, and take someone with you.

—∞—

CHAPTER NINE

Discussion and Reflection

1. The Outward Bound motto is a concise concept: "If you can't get out of it, get into it!" Discuss that motto.
2. Talk about a time when God's voice in the stillness brought a sense of peace. Was that a passage of Scripture, the gentle words of a friend or coach, or a sermon?
3. Read Philippians 2:5-13. Jesus was obedient to death on a cross because of His love for you. What is the only appropriate response? How do you understand the calling of God to take up your cross in following Him?

4. What do you believe are some of the key character qualities that need to be coached in someone who wants to follow Jesus more closely?
5. What spiritual disciplines help you stay on track? What spiritual disciplines are most meaningful for you?
6. What people have modeled servant leadership to you?
7. How might you serve someone this week with a missional mindset?

Alongsider Coaching Challenges

- Plan a spiritual retreat day and reflect on the idea of spiritual disciplines. Try some new and fresh approaches to cultivating your relationship with God. For deeper study, consider Philippians 2:5-11.
- Have a discussion with those you are coaching about the profile of a discipled person, emphasizing the idea of journey and process. Help them take an action step in cross bearing.

—⚬—

CHAPTER TEN

Discussion and Reflection

1. What "cargo" have you had to unload in order to be a more effective coach?
2. An empty truck or a ship without weight can be difficult to pilot. We have a message, a calling, a manifest to deliver to the world. Who have you driven by when you should have stopped along the way? What is your next point of delivery?
3. Read Hebrews 11. Who in that chapter would you like to be your coach and why?
4. Talk about what it means for you to live in the present and embrace the fullness of "now."
5. How would you define "holy listening" and "wholly

listening?"
6. What is your personal mission statement?
7. Who are the friends who are willing to sound the alarm in your life?

Alongsider Coaching Challenges

- Find someone who needs an advocate for a situation they face and encourage him or her. Encourage the people you are coaching to do the same.
- Do an inventory of the things you are carrying. Encourage a person you are walking with to do the same.
- Interact with Hebrews 12:1-3.

━━

CHAPTER ELEVEN

Discussion and Reflection

1. How has God enabled you to soar above the circumstances?
2. Talk about a time when God used you to help someone else soar.
3. Tell about a time when you were in the wrong place spiritually and your "wings were iced over."
4. Who has God placed in your life to help you to take flight for His glory?
5. In what ways have you "flown a long ways?"
6. Talk about the "big rocks," in your life, including those you should be carrying and those that are holding you down.
7. Read James 1:22-25. What decision do you need to pull the trigger on?

Alongsider Coaching Challenges

- Try some alongsider coaching with someone using the pattern of "Ready, Aim, Fire."
- Explain to your coachees the prioritizing analogy of getting the "big rocks" in the cup of their lives.

—∽—

CHAPTER TWELVE
Discussion and Reflection

1. Read Colossians 4:2. Talk about your prayer life. Talk about some of the most significant answers to prayer you have experienced.
2. What is God using from your past to make you who you are today? What things has God used redemptively out of the "junk drawer" of your life?
3. What are the most significant questions you have heard or been asked concerning your prayer life?
4. What are some of your thoughts about how Jesus modeled prayer? If He were your prayer coach, what might He say?
5. Who has taught you the most about prayer? What did they teach you?
6. If you could tell another person the most important things you have learned about prayer, what would be among the things you would say?
7. Describe any "fang time" you have had recently.

Alongsider Coaching Challenges

- Tell someone about your spiritual journey in five minutes or less.
- Pray for workers for the harvest. Fill in some potential names of people who might be an emerging worker.
- Go and make disciples. Listen, ask good questions, tell your story, and pray.

About the Author

Ordained to the ministry with the Christian and Missionary Alliance in 1996, Steve has had a broad base of opportunities which give him practical experience and background in walking alongside others. He has worked in camping ministries, the logging industry, research, ranching, firefighting, and factory work. He served as a soldier in the United States Marine Corps, security guard, furniture delivery man, teacher, special education aid, administrator, missionary teacher overseas, pastor, dorm parent, adjunct faculty at a Bible college, and a church planter. His passion for alongsider coaching fueled his completion of a Doctor of Ministry degree through Fuller Theological Seminary. His work was focused on discipleship coaching. As a pastor, he continues to live out his passion for encouraging and coaching.

If you would like to arrange a training seminar on alongsider coaching for your church or organization, you can contact Steve through his family website, www.thediehls.net.

Acknowledgements

Thanks to Kristi, my best friend and wife. Without her encouragement this work would not have been completed. Thanks to my sons and daughter-in-law, who provided many insights. Thanks to those who have walked with me on the journey of life and helped me in Spirit-led discovery. Thanks to those who helped with editing, including my father and mother. I also want to express gratitude for those who read and endorsed this work. Most of all, thanks to God because He put this project on my heart and fueled the passion to complete it.

NOTES

(Endnotes)

CHAPTER 1

[1] Robert J. Clinton and Laura Raab, *Barnabas: Encouraging Exhorter* (Altadena, CA: Barnabas Publishers, 1997), 47.

CHAPTER 2

[2] Gary Collins, *Christian Coaching; Helping Others Turn Potential into Reality* (Colorado Springs: NavPress, 2001), 32.

[3] Joseph Umidi, *Transformational Coaching* (Virginia Beach, VA: Xulon Press, 2005), 96. Umidi also points out, "When we take a closer look at Jesus the Trainer instead of only Jesus the Teacher, we find that Jesus emphasized transformation over information and even adjusted His equipping to meet the individual needs of learners."

[4] See John 1:38, 2:4, 4:7, 5:6, 6:5, 6:67, 8:10, 10:32, 11:26:b, 13:38a, 18:23, 18:34, 20:15, 21:5, 21:15, 21:16, 21:17, 21:22, 21:23; Matthew 8:26, 9:4-5, 9:28, 11:7-9, 12:11, 15:34, 16:13-15, 17:25, 21:24-25, 22:18-20; Mark 3:4, 3:33, 4:40, 5:30-31, 8:5, 8:17-19, 10:3, 10:36, 11:29-30, 12:15-16; Luke 2:49-49, 8:25, 8:30, 8:45, 9:18-20, 10:36, 14:3, 18:8, 18:41, 20:3-4, 20:24, 22:35, 24:17, 24:38, and Luke 24:41. These passages are great examples of spiritual coaching through strategic questions.

[5] Herbert Lockyer, *All the Men of the Bible* (Grand Rapids: Zondervan, 1958), 52. Lockyer notes, "In the truest sense they were 'no more twain but one.' They were one in their common interest in Christ, and all they accomplished together in the name of the Lord was the result of that perfect unity of a spiritual nature."

CHAPTER 3

[6] Ronald F. Youngblood, *1, 2 Samuel,* Vol. 3, *The Expositor's Bible Commentary* (Edited by Frank E. Gaebelein, Grand Rapids: Zondervan, 1992), 722.

CHAPTER 4

[7] Umidi, *Transformational Coaching,* 56. Umidi suggests a helpful exercise that involves drawing a straight line on a piece of paper. "On the far left of the line write the words 'love to tell,' and the far right, 'love to listen.' As you put a pencil mark along that bar closest to what you really love to do, many will discover that you have been trained towards an addiction to telling!"

[8] Laurie Beth Jones, *Jesus Life Coach* (Nashville: Thomas Nelson, 2004), 211. Jones suggests a distinction between reflective listening and reflexive listening. Reflective listening happens when you intentionally pause to consider what has been said and can repeat it back accurately. Reflexive listening, on the other hand, is waiting simply for your chance to insert something into the conversation.

[9] Susan Scott, *Fierce Conversations* (Nashville: Berkeley Publishing Group, 2002), 223.

CHAPTER 5
[10] Robert E. Logan and Sherilyn Carlton, *Coaching 101* (St. Charles, IL: ChurchSmart Resources, 2003), 101.
[11] 2 Sam. 12:1-7a.

CHAPTER 6
[12] Umidi, *Transformational Coaching*, 26-27.
[13] Ibid., 93.
[14] Erwin McManus, *Seizing Your Divine Moment* (Nashville: Thomas Nelson Publishers, 2002), 41.
[15] *Chariots of Fire*, Enigma Productions, 1981.
[16] Os Guinness, *The Call: Finding and Fulfilling the Central Purpose of Your Life* (Nashville: W Publishing Group, 1998), 34.
[17] Ibid., 71.

CHAPTER 7
[18] Bob Buford, *Game Plan: Winning Strategies for the Second Half of Your Life* (Grand Rapids: Zondervan, 1997), 101.
[19] Marcus Buckingham and Curt Coffman, *First Break All the Rules* (New York: Simon & Schuster, 1999), 153-154.

CHAPTER 8
[20] Lesslie Newbigin, *The Gospel in a Pluralist Society* (London: SPCK, 1989), 227.
[21] Randy Newman, *Stop Answering Questions* (Discipleship Journal, Issue #127), 25.
[22] Matt. 4:19, 8:22, 9:9, 10:38, 16:24, 19:21; Mark 1:17, 2:14, 8:34, 10:21; Luke 5:27, 9:23, 9:59, 14:27, 18:22; John 10:27, 12:26, 21:19, 21:22.

CHAPTER 9
[23] Tim Chester and Steve Timmis, *Total Church* (Crossway Books, 2008), 117-118.
[24] Dallas Willard, *Renovation of the Heart: Putting on the Character of Christ* (Colorado Springs: NavPress, 2002), 53. In this context of denying

oneself and taking up the cross, Willard writes of the difference between self-denial and self-rejection, indicating that they are not the same (pg 61ff).

[25] Randy Alcorn, *The Purity Principle; God's Safeguards for Life's Dangerous Trails* (Multnomah Books, 2003), 17.

[26] Umidi, *Transformational Coaching,* 79.

[27] Donald O. Clifton and Paula Nelson, *Soar with Your Strengths* (New York: Dell Trade Paperback, 1992), 31. On page 16 the authors write, "Trying to succeed in an area in which you are weak will lead to a negative self-concept." I have wrestled with this in the past, and see it as a helpful warning for a young coachee.

[28] Ibid., 42.

[29] Ibid.,19.

[30] Reggie McNeal, DMin class lecture in "OD755: Developing Self-Understanding and Ministry Health," Fuller Theological Seminary, August 2004.

[31] Richard Clinton and Paul Leavenworth, *Starting Well* (Altadena, CA: Barnabas Publishers, 1994), 125.

[32] Marcus Buckingham and Donald O. Clifton, *Now, Discover Your Strengths* (New York: The Free Press, 2001), 61. Identifying these talents, according to the authors on page 67ff, is a process of monitoring your "spontaneous, top-of-mind reactions" to the situations you encounter, tuning in to "yearnings" that reveal the presence of a talent, watching for areas of "rapid learning," and being aware of "satisfactions" that are the result of activities and behaviors.

[33] Ibid., 75. This is a strongly suggested book for use with the equipping of emerging workers. The online strengths assessment that accompanies this book is highly valuable.

[34] Umidi, *Transformational Coaching,* 55. Umidi refers to this as "divine masterpiece."

[35] Clifton and Nelson, *Soar with Your Strengths,* 73.

[36] Avery T. Willis Jr. and Kay Moore, *The Disciple's Cross* (Nashville: LifeWay Press, 1996).

[37] John C. Maxwell, *Developing the Leaders Around You: How to Help Others Reach Their Full Potential.* (Nashville: Thomas Nelson Publishers, 1995), 47-48.

[38] Umidi, *Transformational Coaching,* 214.

[39] Bradford A. Mullen, Class lecture in the course, "Hermeneutics: History and Issues, Bible 605," Columbia Bible College and Seminary, October 29, 1992.

[40] Reggie McNeal, *Revolution in Leadership: Training Apostles for Tomorrow's Church* (Nashville: Abingdon Press, 1998), 41.

[41] Maxwell, *Developing the Leaders Around You: How to Help Others Reach Their Full Potential, 2.*

[42] David E. Schroeder, *Follow Me: The Master's Plan for Men* (Grand Rapids: Baker Book House, 1992), 24.
[43] Bill Thrall, Bruce McNicol, and John Lynch, *True Faced: Trust God and Others with Who You Really Are* (Colorado Springs: NavPress, 2003), 196.
[44] Bill Mowry, *The Ways of the Alongsider* (Bill Mowry, 2011), 3.

CHAPTER 10
[45] Andy Stanley, *Next Generation Leader; Five Essentials for Those Who will Shape the Future.* (Multnomah Books 2003), 104.
[46] Laurie Beth Jones, *Jesus Life Coach* (Nashville: Thomas Nelson, 2004), 229.
[47] James Flaherty, *Coaching: Evoking Excellence in Others* (Burlington, MA: Butterworth Heinemann, 2005), 11.
[48] Schroeder, *Follow Me: The Master's Plan for Men*, 32.
[49] Mary Dee Hicks and David Peterson, *Leader as Coach* (Minneapolis: Personnel Decision International, 1996), 117.
[50] Umidi, *Transformational Coaching,* 174.
[51] Keith R. Anderson and Randy Reese, *Spiritual Mentoring: A Guide for Seeking and Giving Direction* (Downers Grove, IL: InterVarsity Press, 1999), 90.
[52] Mary Brounstein, *Coaching and Mentoring for Dummies* (New York: Wiley Publishing, 2000), 128.
[53] Erwin McManus, *Seizing Your Divine Moment* (Nashville: Thomas Nelson Publishers, 2002), 18.
[54] Brounstein, *Coaching and Mentoring for Dummies*, 13.
[55] Reggie McNeal, *Revolution in Leadership: Training Apostles for Tomorrow's Church.* (Nashville: Abingdon Press, 1998), 41.
[56] McManus, *Seizing Your Divine Moment,* 142.
[57] Hicks and Peterson, *Leader as Coach,* 14.
[58] Brounstein, *Coaching and Mentoring for Dummies*, 69.
[59] Ibid., 33.
[60] Maxwell, *Developing the Leaders Around You: How to Help Others Reach Their Full Potential,* 125.
[61] Susan Scott, *Fierce Conversations* (Nashville: Berkeley Publishing Group, 2002), 155.
[62] Ibid., 154.
[63] Ibid., 7.
[64] Ibid., 31.

CHAPTER 11
[65] Hicks and Peterson, *Leader as Coach,* 29.
[66] Ibid., 32.

[67] Ibid., 18-19.
[68] Mowry, *The Ways of the Alongsider*, 57.
[69] Ibid., 57.
[70] Jones, *Jesus Life Coach*, 51.

CHAPTER 12
[71] James L. Nicodem , *Prayer Coach* (Wheaton, Illinois: Crossway Books, 2008), 69.
[72] Willard, *Hearing God: Developing a Conversational Relationship with God*, 33.

LIFEHOUSE PUBLISHING

Bringing Life to Books

Do you need a speaker?

Do you want Steven L. Diehl to speak to your group or event?
Then contact Larry Davis at: **(623) 337-8710** or email:
ldavis@intermediapr.com or use the contact form at:
www.lifehousepub.com

Whether you want to purchase bulk copies of *Alongsider
Coaching* or buy another book for a friend, get it now at:
www.lifehousepub.com
If you have a book that you would like to publish,
contact Terry Whalin, Publisher, at Lifehouse Publishing
Group, (623) 337-8710 or
email: **twhalin@intermediapub.com**
or use the contact form at:**www.lifehousepub.com**